AN INTERPRETATION OF CHRISTIAN ETHICS

AN INTERPRETATION OF CHRISTIAN ETHICS

Reinhold Niebuhr

1817

Harper & Row, Publishers, San Francisco

Cambridge, Hagerstown, New York, Philadelphia, Washington
London, Mexico City, São Paulo, Singapore, Sydney

Library of Congress Cataloging-in-Publication Data

Neibuhr, Reinhold, 1892–1971.
  An interpretation of Christian ethics.
  Includes bibliographical references and index.
  1. Christian ethics. 2. Love (Theology)
I. Title.
BJ1251.N5 1987   241   86-31935
ISBN 0-8164-2206-0

87 88 89 90 91   10 9 8 7 6 5

CONTENTS

PREFACE

The substance of these chapters was presented as the Rausch-enbusch Memorial Lectures at Colgate-Rochester Divinity School in the spring of 1934. Their substance unfortunately did not offer as large an opportunity as might be desirable to come to grips with the dominant note in Rauschenbusch's theology. I venture to hope however that they are an extension and an application to our own day of both the social realism and the loyalty to the Christian faith which characterized the thought and life of one who was not only the real founder of social Christianity in this country but also its most brilliant and generally satisfying exponent to the present day.

I should like to express my gratitude to the president and faculty of The Colgate-Rochester Divinity School for the gener-ous sympathy with which they received the lecturer and his message and for the privilege of speaking on a foundation which promises to make a unique contribution to the cause of social Christianity in this country. I also owe a particular debt of gratitude to my colleague, Professor Paul Tillich, for many valuable suggestions in the development of my theme, some of them made specifically and others the by-product of innumera-ble discussions on the thesis of this book.

Reinhold Niebuhr

Union Theological Seminary
New York City

1

AN INDEPENDENT
CHRISTIAN ETHIC

Protestant Christianity in America is, unfortunately, unduly dependent upon the very culture of modernity, the disintegration of which would offer a more independent religion a unique opportunity. Confused and tormented by cataclysmic events in contemporary history, the "modern mind" faces the disintegration of its civilization in alternate moods of fear and hope, of faith and despair. The culture of modernity was the artifact of modern civilization, product of its unique and characteristic conditions, and it is therefore not surprising that its minarets of the spirit should fall when the material foundations of its civilization begin to crumble. Its optimism had no more solid foundation than the expansive mood of the era of triumphant capitalism and naturally gives way to confusion and despair when the material conditions of life are seriously altered. Therefore the lights in its towers are extinguished at the very moment when light is needed to survey the havoc wrought in the city and the plan of rebuilding.

At such a time a faith which claims to have a light, "the same yesterday, today, and forever," might conceivably become a source of illumination to its age, so sadly in need of clues to the meaning of life and the logic of contemporary history. The Christian churches are, unfortunately, not able to offer the needed guidance and insight. The orthodox churches have long since compounded the truth of the Christian religion with dogmatisms of another day, and have thereby petrified what would otherwise have long since fallen prey to the beneficent dissolutions of the processes of nature and history. The liberal churches, on the other hand, have hid their light under the bushel of the culture of modernity with all its short-lived prejudices and presumptuous certainties.

To be more specific: Orthodox Christianity, with insights and perspectives, in many ways superior to those of liberalism, cannot come to the aid of modern man, partly because its religious truths are still imbedded in an outmoded science and partly because its morality is expressed in dogmatic and authoritarian moral codes. It tries vainly to meet the social perplexities of a complex civilization with irrelevant precepts, deriving their authority from their—sometimes quite fortuitous—inclusion in a sacred canon. It concerns itself with the violation of Sabbatarian prohibitions or puritanical precepts, and insists, figuratively, on tithing "mint, anise, and cummin," preserving the minutiae of social and moral standards which may once have had legitimate or accidental sanctity, but which have, whether legitimate or accidental, now lost both religious and moral meaning.

The religion and ethics of the liberal church are dominated by the desire to prove to its generation that it does not share the anachronistic ethics or believe the incredible myths of orthodox religion. Its energy for some decades has been devoted to the task of proving religion and science compatible, a purpose which it has sought to fulfil by disavowing the more incredible portion of its religious heritage and clothing the remainder in terms acceptable to the "modern mind." It has discovered rather belatedly that this same modern mind, which only yesterday seemed to be the final arbiter of truth, beauty, and goodness, is in a sad state of confusion today, amidst the debris of the shattered temple of its dreams and hopes. In adjusting itself to the characteristic credos and prejudices of modernity, the liberal church has been in constant danger of obscuring what is distinctive in the Christian message and creative in Christian morality. Sometimes it fell to the level of merely clothing the naturalistic philosophy and the utilitarian ethics of modernity with pious phrases.

The distinctive contribution of religion to morality lies in its comprehension of the dimension of depth in life. A secular moral act resolves the conflicts of interest and passion, revealed in any immediate situation, by whatever counsels a decent prudence may suggest, the most usual counsel being that of moderation—"in nothing too much." A religious morality is constrained by its sense of a dimension of depth to trace every force with which it deals to some ultimate origin and to relate every purpose to some ultimate end. It is concerned not only with immediate values and disvalues, but with the problem of good and evil, not only with immediate objectives, but with ultimate hopes. It is troubled by the question of the primal "whence" and the final "wherefore." It is troubled by these questions because religion is concerned with life and existence as a unity and coherence of meaning. In so far as it is impossible to live at all without presupposing a meaningful existence, the life of every person is religious, with the possible exception of the rare sceptic who is more devoted to the observation of life than to living it, and whose interest in detailed facts is more engrossing than his concern for ultimate meaning and coherence. Even such persons have usually constructed a little cosmos in a world which they regard as chaos and derive vitality and direction from their faith in organizing purpose of this cosmos.

High religion is distinguished from the religion of both primitives and ultra-moderns by its effort to bring the whole of reality and existence into some system of coherence. The primitives, on the other hand, are satisfied by some limited cosmos, and the moderns by a superficial one. For primitive man the unity of the tribe or the majesty and mystery of some natural force—the sun, the moon, the mountain, or the generative process—may be the sacred centre of a meaningful existence. For modern man the observable sequences of natural law or the supposedly increasing values of human co-operation are sufficient to establish a sense of spiritual security and to banish the fear of chaos and meaninglessness which has beset the human spirit throughout the ages.

This straining after an ultimate coherence inevitably drives high religion into depth as well as breadth; for the forms of life are too various and multifarious to be ascribed easily to a single source or related to a single realm of meaning if the source does not transcend all the observable facts and forces, and the realm does not include more than the history of the concrete world. The problem of evil and incoherence cannot be solved on the plane on which the incompatible forces and incommensurate realities (thought and extension, man and nature, spirit and matter) remain in stubborn conflict or rational incompatibility. Since all life is dynamic, religious faith seeks for the solution of the problem of evil by centering its gaze upon the beginning and the end of this dynamic process, upon God the creator and God the fulfillment of existence. Invariably it identifies the origin and source with the goal and end as belonging to the same realm of reality, a proposition which involves religion in many rational difficulties but remains, nevertheless, a perennial and necessary affirmation.

High religions are thus distinguished by the extent of the unity and coherence of life which they seek to encompass and the sense of a transcendent source of meaning by which alone confidence in the meaningfulness of life and existence can be maintained. The dimension of depth in religion is not created simply by the effort to solve the problem of unity in the total breadth of life. The dimension of depth is really prior to any experience of breadth; for the assumption that life is meaningful and that its meaning transcends the observable facts of existence is involved in all achievements of knowledge by which life in its richness and contradictoriness is apprehended. Yet the effort to establish coherence and meaning in terms of breadth increases the sense of depth. Thus the God of a primitive tribe is conceived as the transcendent source of its life; and faith in such a God expresses the sense of the unity and value of tribal solidarity. But when experience forces an awakening culture to fit the life of other peoples into its world, it conceives of a God who transcends the life of one people so completely as no longer to be bound to it. Thus a prophet Amos arises to declare, "Are ye not as the children of the Ethiopians unto me sayeth the Lord." What is divided, incompatible, and conflicting, on the plane of concrete history is felt to be united, harmonious, and akin in its common source ("God hath made of one blood all the nations of men") and its common destiny ("In Christ there is neither Jew nor Greek, neither bond nor free").

The dimension of depth in the consciousness of religion creates the tension between what is and what ought to be. It bends the bow from which every arrow of moral action flies. Every truly moral act seeks to establish what ought to be, because the agent feels obligated to the ideal, though historically unrealized, as being the order of life in its more essential reality. Thus the Christian believes that the ideal of love is real in the will and nature of God, even though he knows of no place in history where the ideal has been realized in its pure form. And it is because it has this reality that he feels the pull of obligation. The sense of obligation in morals from which Kant tried to derive the whole structure of religion is really derived from the religion itself. The "pull" or "drive" of moral life is a part of the religious tension of life. Man seeks to realize in history what he conceives to be already the truest reality—that is, its final essence.

The ethical fruitfulness of various types of religion is determined by the quality of their tension between the historical and the transcendent. This quality is measured by two considerations: The degree to which the transcendent truly transcends every value and achievement of history, so that no relative value of historical achievement may become the basis of moral complacency; and the degree to which the transcendent remains in organic contact with the historical, so that no degree of tension may rob the historical of its significance.

The weakness of orthodox Christianity lies in its premature identification of the transcendent will of God with canonical moral codes, many of which are merely primitive social standards, and for development of its myths into a bad science. The perennial tendency of religion to identify God with the symbols of God in history, symbols which were once filled with a sanctity, of which the stream of new events and conditions has robbed them, is a perpetual source of immorality in religion. The failure of liberal Christianity is derived from its inclination to invest the relative moral standards of a commercial age with ultimate sanctity by falsely casting the aura of the absolute and transcendent ethic of Jesus upon them. A religion which capitulates to the prejudices of a contemporary age is not very superior to a religion which remains enslaved to the partial and relative insights of an age already dead. In each case religion fails because it prematurely resolves moral tension by discovering, or claiming to have realized, the *summum bonum* in some immediate and relative value of history. The whole of modern secular liberal culture, to which liberal Christianity is unduly bound, is really a devitalized and secularized religion in which the presuppositions of a Christian tradition have been rationalized and read into the processes of history and nature, supposedly discovered by objective science. The original tension of Christian morality is thereby destroyed; for the transcendent ideals of Christian morality have become immanent possibilities in the historic process. Democracy, mutual co-operation, the League of Nations, international trade reciprocity, and other similar conceptions are regarded as the ultimate ideals of the human spirit. None of them are without some degree of absolute validity, but modern culture never discovered to what degree they had emerged out of the peculiar conditions and necessities of a commercial civilization and were intimately related to the interests of the classes which have profited most by the expansion of commerce and industry in recent decades. The transcendent impossibilities of the Christian ethic of love became, in modern culture, the immanent and imminent possibilities of an historical process; and the moral complacence of a generation is thereby supported rather than challenged. This is the invariable consequence of any culture in which no "windows are left open to heaven" and the experience of depth in life is completely dissipated by a confident striving along the horizontal line of the immediate stream of history.

The accommodation of the modern church to a secular culture was so necessary that its occasional capitulation can be understood sympathetically, however baneful the consequences may have been. Medieval Christianity had resisted the advance of science and supported a dying feudal order against the rebellion of a rationalistic morality. The limitations of traditional religion were so great and the achievements of modern science so impressive that it seemed the better part of wisdom to relate the Christian enterprise as intimately as possible with the latter. Whatever its weaknesses, this strategy served at least one good purpose in emancipating Christianity from dogmatic and literalistic interpretations of its mythical inheritance. The genius of religious myth at its best is that it is trans-scientific. Its peril is to express itself in pre-scientific concepts and insist on their literal truth. If liberal religion had not admitted science (in the form of a critico-historical analysis of its sources) into the very heart of the church it would have been impossible to free what is eternal in the Christian religion from the shell of an outmoded culture in which it had become embedded.

Nevertheless, the loss suffered by liberal Christianity's too uncritical accommodation to modern culture was very great. Its extent is only now becoming apparent when the culture, which had discredited religion because its literally interpreted myths resulted in a bad science, is being in turn discredited because the unrevised philosophical implications of a mere scientific description of historic facts result in a thin and superficial religion. The mythical symbols of transcendence in profound religion are easily corrupted into scientifically untrue statements of historic fact. But the scientific description of historic sequences may be as easily corrupted into an untrue conception of total reality. It is the genius of true myth to suggest the dimension of depth in reality and to point to a realm of essence which transcends the surface of history, on which the cause-effect sequences, discovered and analysed by science, occur. Science can only deal with this surface of nature and history, analysing, dividing, and segregating its detailed phenomena and relating them to each other in terms of their observable sequences. In its effort to bring coherence into its world it can escape the error of a too mechanistic view of reality only with the greatest difficulty and at the price of philosophical corrections of philosophical assumptions unconsciously implied in its method. It is bound to treat each new emergent in history as having its adequate cause in an antecedent event in history, thus committing the logical fallacy, *Post hoc, ergo propter hoc.*

The religious myth, on the other hand, points to the ultimate ground of existence and its ultimate fulfilment. Therefore the great religious myths deal with creation and redemption. But since myth cannot speak of the trans-historical without using symbols and events in history as its form of expression, it invariably falsifies the facts of history, as seen by science, to state its truth. Religion must therefore make the confession of St Paul its own: "As deceivers and yet true" (2 Cor. vi. 8). If in addition religion should insist that its mythical devices have a sacred authority which may defy the conclusions at which science arrives through its observations, religion is betrayed into deception without truth.

Philosophy is, in a sense, a mediator between science and religion. It seeks to bring the religious myth into terms of rational coherence, with all the detailed phenomena of existence which science discloses. Bertrand Russell's indictment of metaphysics as covert theology remains true even if the modern metaphysician seeks to dispense with religious presuppositions and to act as a co-ordinator of the sciences. He cannot relate all the detailed facts revealed by science into a total scheme of coherence without presuppositions which are not suggested by the scientific description of the facts, but which are consciously or unconsciously introduced by a religiously grounded world-view.

If theology is an effort to construct a rational and systematic view of life out of the various and sometimes contradictory myths which are associated with a single religious tradition, philosophy carries the process one step farther by seeking to dispense with the mythical basis altogether and resting its world-view entirely upon the ground of rational consistency. Thus for Hegel, religion is no more than primitive philosophy in terms of crude picture-thinking, which a more advanced rationality refines. This rationalization of myth is indeed inevitable and necessary, lest religion be destroyed by undisciplined and fantastic imagery or primitive and inconsistent myth. Faith must feed on reason (Unamuno). But reason must also feed on faith. Every authentic religious myth contains paradoxes of the relation between the finite and the eternal which cannot be completely rationalized without destroying the genius of true religion. Metaphysics is therefore more dependent upon, and more perilous to, the truth in the original religious myth than is understood in a rationalistic and scientific culture.[1]

It was apparent neither to modern culture nor to modern Christianity that the unconscious moral and religious compla-

---

[1] Berdyaev has an interesting word on the validity of myths: "Myth is a reality immeasurably greater than concept. It is high time that we stopped identifying myth with invention, with the illusions of primitive mentality. . . . Behind the myths are concealed the greatest realities, the original phenomena of the spiritual life. . . . Myth is always concrete and expresses life better than abstract thought can do. . . . Myth presents to us the supernatural in the natural—it brings two worlds together symbolically."—(*Freedom and the Spirit*, p. 70.)

cence of the bourgeois soul was as influential in discrediting religious myth as the scientific criticism of religious mythology. Modern culture is compounded of the genuine achievements of science and the peculiar ethos of a commercial civilization. The superficialities of the latter, its complacent optimism, its loss of the sense of depth and the knowledge of good and evil (the heights of good and the depths of evil) were at least as influential in it if not more influential than the discoveries of science. Therefore the adjustment of modern religion to the "mind" of modern culture inevitably involved capitulation to its thin "soul." Liberal Christianity, in adjusting itself to the ethos of this age, therefore sacrificed its most characteristic religious and Christian heritage by destroying the sense of depth and the experience of tension, typical of profound religion. Its Kingdom of God was translated to mean exactly that ideal society which modern culture hoped to realize through the evolutionary process. Democracy and the League of Nations were to be the political forms of this ideal. The Christian ideal of love became the counsel of prudential mutuality so dear and necessary to a complex commercial civilization. The Christ of Christian orthodoxy, true mythical symbol of both the possibilities and the limits of the human, became the good man of Galilee, symbol of human goodness and human possibilities without suggestion of the limits of the human and the temporal—in short, without the suggestion of transcendence. — Access w/o Transcendance.

Failure to recognize the heights led modern Christianity to an equal blindness toward the darker depths of life. The "sin" of Christian orthodoxy was translated into the imperfections of ignorance, which an adequate pedagogy would soon overcome. Hence the difference between a Christian education, teaching the religious ideal of love, and a secular education intent upon enlarging social imagination, became imperceptible. There has been little suggestion in modern culture of the demonic force in human life, of the peril in which all achievements of life and civilization constantly stand because the evil impulses in men may be compounded in collective actions until they reach diabolical proportions; or of the dark and turgid impulses, imbedded in the unconscious of the individual and defying and mocking his conscious control and his rational moral pretensions. Modern culture, both Christian and secular, was optimistic enough to believe that all the forces which determine each moral and social situation were fully known and completely understood, and that the forces of reason had successfully chained all demonic powers.

It is by faith in transcendence that a profound religion is saved from complete capitulation to the culture of any age, past or present. When modern Christianity, confused by the prestige of science, the temper of a this-worldly age and the disrepute of orthodox dogmatism, sought to come to terms with current naturalism, it lost the power to penetrate into the ethical aberrations and confusions of a naturalistic culture and to correct its superficiality and false optimism.

It is significant for the history of modern Christianity that the more realistic portion of the church which recognizes the weaknesses and limitations of a liberal culture, inclines to substitute a radical Marxian world-view for the discarded liberal one. That disillusionment over the weaknesses of liberalism should lead Christian radicalism to substitute Marxian catastrophism for liberal optimism is in itself commendable. However, the tendency in America is for Christian radicalism to be dissolved in Marxian radicalism. This tendency is particularly strong in America because the morally vigorous section of the Church in this country has been secularized by modern culture to a much larger degree than in any other Western nation. American Protestantism is superficially more influential than the Church in other nations, but its roots are not so deep in the traditions of historic Christianity. It is consequently more prone to a premature disavowal of the characteristic concepts and the moral and religious tension of historic Christianity.

The attachment of radical Christianity to Marxian viewpoints, even though on occasion unqualified, represents a gain in religious as well as moral realism. But Marxism is as naturalistic as modern liberalism. It is therefore deficient in an ultimate perspective upon historic and relative moral achievements. It is as prone to identify the characteristic attitudes and values of the workers with the absolute truth as is liberalism to identify the bourgeois perspectives with eternal values. Both liberalism and Marxism are secularized and naturalized versions of the Hebrew prophetic movement and the Christian religion. But Marxism is a purer derivative of the prophetic movement. Its materialism is "dialetic" rather than mechanistic; and the dialectic (*i.e.*, the logic of thesis, antithesis, and synthesis) is much truer to the complex facts of history than the simple evolutionary process of liberal naturalism. It has a better understanding of the depths of evil which reveal themselves in human history, and hence its philosophy of history contains a catastrophism, completely foreign to the dominant mood of modern culture, but closely related to the catastrophism of Jewish prophecy ("The day of the Lord will be darkness and not light," declared the prophet Amos). In common with apocalyptic religion it transmutes an immediate pessimism into an ultimate optimism by its hope in the final establishment of an ideal social order through a miracle of history. In the case of Marxism the proletariat is the active agent of this consummation; yet its success would be impossible without the activity of God, who casts the mighty from their seats and exalts them of low degree. Since Marxism is a secularized religion the divine activity takes the form of a logic of history which preordains that the mighty shall destroy themselves and shall give political strength to the weak in their very effort to destroy them. (This Marxian conception is incidentally the fruit of both a profound religious feeling and of astute social observations. The paradoxes of high religion are in it and the actual facts of history substantiate it to a considerable degree.)

The weakness of the Marxian apocalypse is that its naturalism betrays it into utopian fantasies. Whenever naturalism appropriates the mythical symbols in religion of the unconditioned and transcendent, to make them goals in time and history, it falsely expects the realization of an absolute ideal in the relative temporal process. The anarchistic millennium of Marxism, where each will give according to his ability and take according to his need, in which all social conflicts will be finally resolved and all human needs satisfied, is the perfect product of a naturalistic religion which tries vainly to domesticate the eternal and absolute and to fit the vision of perfection into the inevitable imperfections of history.

Utopianism must inevitably lead to disillusionment. Naturalistic apocalypse is unable to maintain the moral tension which it has created. It has no means of discovering that its visions and dreams are relative to partial interests and temporary perspectives and that even the universal element in them will lose its universality and unqualifiedness when it is made concrete in history. Moral tension thus degenerates into moral complacency when the relative historical achievement is accepted as the ideal. Both liberal and radical naturalism have moral beauty when they are waiting for their "word" to "become flesh," but they are betrayed into lethargy and hypocrisy after the incarnation.

This spiritual decay is a matter of historical record in liberal bourgeois culture. It can be gauged with historical precision by comparing the dreams of the Age of Reason, of a Godwin, a Diderot, a Rousseau, or even an Adam Smith with the pathetic inanities by which twentieth-century idealists seek to give spiritual dignity to the sorry realities of a brutal capitalistic civilization. A perfect symbol of the contrast in an abbreviated span of history is found in the Wilson who conceived the vision of a warless world and a League of Nations and the Wilson who tried to make himself believe that the treaty of Versailles approximated his ideals.

Radical spirituality has the present advantage of still living in the pre- rather than post-apocalypse period of its ideals. Only in Russia, where the ideal has become history, can one observe the beginning of this decay, though the years are too brief to assess it truly. The difference between Lenin's complete sincerity and Stalin's cynical statecraft establishes the tangent which, one may confidently predict, history will further elaborate. Another aspect of the same contrast is Trotsky's fierce enthusiasm for a world revolution and Stalin's prudent contraction of the revolutionary ideal so that it may be compounded with Russian patriotism and harnessed to specifically Russian political and economic tasks. Perhaps Stalin is related to Trotsky as was Napoleon to Rousseau.

A Christianity which leans unduly on or borrows excessively from naturalistic idealism, whether liberal or radical, is really betrayed into dependence upon corruptions of its own ethos and culture. The significance of Hebrew-Christian religion lies in the fact that the tension between the ideal and the real which it creates can be maintained at any point in history, no matter what the moral and social achievement, because its ultimate ideal always transcends every historical fact and reality.

It is significant for the character of Western spirituality that it is tempted to destroy religious tension by losing the transcendent in the historical process and not, as in Eastern religion, by making the transcendent irrelevant to the historical process. Modern naturalism, whether liberal or radical, is a secularized version of the naturalistic element in historic Hebrew-Christian mythology. It is important to recognize that the God of Hebrew and Christian faith is the creator of the world, as well as its judge, and that according to this faith the ultimate meaning of life is both revealed in and corrupted by the temporal process. While the temper of the Western World tends to dissolve the paradoxical dialectic of this faith in the direction of a naturalism which dissipates the element of perpetual transcendence, it is important to remember that the spiritual and moral loss is just as great if reaction to naturalism drives Christianity into an other-worldly dualism in which the transcendent ceases to have relevance to the historical and temporal process.

If we are to mark out the true dimensions of an independent Christian ethic we must, therefore, be as careful to disassociate it from idealistic dualisms as from naturalistic monisms. The determining characteristic of all dualistic religion is that in its effort to escape the relativity of the temporal and material it finds escape in some rational or eternal absolute, in a realm of the supernatural which ceases to be the ground of the natural, but is only the ultimate abyss of the natural where all distinctions vanish and all dynamic processes cease.

Söderblom divides all higher religions into religions of culture and religions of revelation, placing Christianity and Judaism alone (and possibly Zoroastrianism) in the latter category.[1] The distinguishing mark of culture religions is that they seek by some rational or mystical discipline to penetrate to the eternal forms which transcend temporal reality. The distinctive feature of a religion of revelation (also defined as prophetic religion) is that "its contrast is not that of spirit versus bodily form, but rather that of Creator above the created, the living jealous God above every image or likeness."[2] The myth of creation offers, in other words, the firm foundation for a world-view which sees the Transcendent involved in, but not identified with, the process of history. It is important to realize that the myth of creation is only the basis of

[1] Nathan Söderblom, *The Nature of Revelation*, pp. 1-56.
[2] *Ibid.*, p. 61.

this dialectic and that its further elaboration results in the prophetic or apocalyptic characteristic of this religion, marked by its hope for an ultimate fulfilment of meaning and its faith that the God who is the ground of existence is also the guarantor of its fulfilment. In making practically the same distinction and contrast as that of Söderblom, John Oman declares "the term apocalyptic is used in contrast to the mystic and means any religion which looks for an unveiling of the supernatural in the natural."[1]

Perhaps the distinction between the two types of religion could be most accurately expressed by the terms "mystical" and "mythical." The "religions of culture" of Söderblom's category are ultimately mystical though immediately rational. They begin by a rational quest after the eternal forms within the passing flux. But rational observations turns into mystical contemplation as it strains after the final vision of the absolute and eternal. The eternal forms which give body to temporal reality finally become disassociated from it; and the eternal becomes an undifferentiated transcendence, "a fathomless depth in which no distinctions are visible or a fullness of being that exceeds our comprehension."[2] The ultimate consequence of this method of apprehending the absolute may be seen in Buddhism most clearly; but every mystical religion portrays the tendencies. The mystical is the rational in its final effort to transcend the temporal, an effort which forces it to transcend even the rational. The mystical carries the rational passion for unity and coherence to the point where the eye turns from the outward scene, with its recalcitrant facts and stubborn variety, to the inner world of spirit, where the unity of self-consciousness becomes the symbol of and the means of reaching, the Absolute, a type of reality which is "beyond existence," "a mysterious silent stillness which dissolves consciousness and form" (Hierotheus). Thus religion, seeking after the final source of life's meaning and its organizing centre, ends by destroying the meaning of life. Historic and concrete existence is robbed of its meaning because its temporal and relative forms are believed not worthy to be compared with the Absolute; but the Absolute is also bereft of meaning because it transcends every form and category of concrete existence. Mysticism is really a

---

[1] John Oman, *The Natural and the Supernatural*, p. 427.
[2] Morris Cohen, *Reason and Nature*, p. 146.

self-devouring rationalism which begins by abstracting rational forms from concrete reality and ends by positing an ultimate reality beyond all rational forms.

It must not be assumed that rationalism must always end in mysticism. The idealistic monism of the Western World, from Plato to Hegel, represents the effort of a more sober type of rationalism to comprehend the unity of the world within the living flux of history. As far as it succeeds in doing this it results in the optimistic identification of the Absolute with the totality of things, a conclusion at variance with tragic realities of existence and detrimental to high moral passion. While the Western World has, on the whole, tended to satisfy the rationalistic yearning after the ultimate unity with philosophical monisms, which complicate the problem of evil, the Oriental World (perhaps because it is older and wiser or because it is more disillusioned) has chosen the more dualistic and pessimistic alternative and has found its ultimate unity and centre of meaning only after fleeing the temporal world completely. Even in the Western World, noticeably in Christian mysticism, the robust but also romantic optimism of monistic philosophy is easily transmuted into a pessimistic other-worldliness. The road from Plato to Plotinus and Neo-Platonism marks this path.

Whether rationalistic religion tends toward the optimism of philosophical monism or the pessimism of dualistic mysticism, it is an essentially aristocratic religion, unavailable for the burden-bearers of the world. These cannot indulge in the luxury of the contemplative withdrawal from the world which such religion requires; nor does the curious mixture of beauty and tragedy revealed and enacted in their lives permit them to harbour the illusions of either pure pessimism or pure optimism.

While Christianity has been partly formed and certainly influenced by rational and mystical religions, it owes its primary basis to a mythical rather than a mystical religious heritage—that of the Hebrew prophetic movement. Myths are not peculiar to Hebrew religion. They are to be found in the childhood of every culture when the human imagination plays freely upon the rich variety of facts and events in life and history, and seeks to discover their relation to basic causes and ultimate meanings without a careful examination of their relation to each other in the realm of natural causation. In this sense mythical thinking is simply pre-scientific thinking, which has not learned to analyse the relation of things to each other before fitting them into its picture of the whole. Perhaps the simplest mythical thought is the animistic thought of the primitives in which each phenomenon of the natural world is related to a quasi-conscious or quasi-spiritual causal force with little or no understanding of the web of cause-effect relationships in the natural world itself. But mythical thought is not only pre-scientific; it is also supra-scientific. It deals with vertical aspects of reality which transcend the horizontal relationships which science analyses, charts and records. The classical myth refers to the transcendent source and end of existence without abstracting it from existence.

In this sense the myth alone is capable of picturing the world as a realm of coherence and meaning without defying the facts of incoherence. Its world is coherent because all facts in it are related to some central source of meaning, but is not rationally coherent because the myth is not under the abortive necessity of relating all things to each other in terms of immediate rational unity. The God of mythical religion is, significantly, the Creator and not the First Cause. If he were first cause (a rational conception) he would be either one of the many observable causes in the stream of things, in which case God and the world are one; or he would be the unmoved mover, in which case his relation to the world is not a vital or truly creative one. To say that God is the creator is to use an image which transcends the canons of rationality, but which expresses both his organic relation to the world and his distinction from the world. To believe that God created the world is to feel that the world is a realm of meaning and coherence without insisting that the world is totally good or that the totality of things must be identified with the Sacred. The myth of the creator God is basic to Hebraic religion. The significant achievement of the prophetic movement in Hebraic religion is that it was able to purge its religion of the parochial and puerile weaknesses of its childhood without rationalizing it and thus destroying the virtue of its myth. The purifying process in Hebraic religion through which it arrived at a pure monotheism was dominated by an ethico-religious passion rather than a rational urge for consistency. It therefore increased the width and extent of its meaningful world until it included the whole of existence without destroying the sense of depth and transcendence. In this dimension of depth it had room for evil without attributing it to either God or to the material world. In the myth of the fall, the origin of sin is not made identical with the genesis of life. It is therefore not synonymous with creation, either in the sense that God ordained it or that it is the inevitable consequence of the incarnation of spirit in matter and nature. Hebrew spirituality was, consequently, never corrupted by either the optimism which conceived the world as possessing unqualified sanctity and goodness or the pessimism which relegated historic existence to a realm of meaningless cycles. The existence of evil was, on the one hand, a mystery, and was, on the other hand (perhaps too unqualifiedly), attributed to human perversity. The myth of the fall makes the latter explanation too unqualifiedly in the sense that it derives all the inadequacies of nature from man's disobedience, a rather too sweeping acceptance of human responsibility for nature's ruthlessness and for the brevity and mortality of natural life.

The mythical basis of the Hebraic world-view enables Hebraic spirituality to enjoy the pleasures of this life without becoming engrossed in them, and to affirm the significance of human history without undue reverence for the merely human. In the Hebraic world both nature and history glorify the Creator: "The heavens declare the glory of God and the firmament showeth his handiwork," and "O Lord, how manifold are thy works! in wisdom hast thou made them all. The earth is full of thy riches." Such sentiments abound in the devotional literature of the Jews. The second Isaiah, whose prophetic insights lift Hebraic religion to its sublimest heights, finds the majesty of God in both his creative nearness to and his distance from the created world. God speaks to him as follows: "I am the Lord and there is none else. I make the peace and create evil. I the Lord do all these things. Woe unto him who strivest with his maker. Shall the clay say to him that fashioneth it, What makest thou?—Verily thou art a God that *hidest thyself*, O God of Israel the Saviour" (Isa. xlv.). Or again, "It is he that sitteth on the circle of the earth, and the inhabitants thereof are as grasshoppers; that stretcheth out the heavens as a curtain and spreadeth them out as a tent to dwell in" (Isa. xl.). In these sublime mythical conceptions God is revealed in the creation because he is the creator, but he also transcends the world as the creator and his transcendence reaches to a height where it defies comprehension ("Thou art a God that hidest thyself").

The myth of the Creator God offers the possibilities for a prophetic religion in which the transcendent God becomes both the judge and the redeemer of the world. This possibility is, however, not an inevitability. It is always possible that a mythical religion become unduly centred in the myth of Genesis, thus glorifying the given world as sacred without subjecting its imperfections to the judgment of the Holy. In this case the result is a religion of sacramentalism rather than of prophecy. The sacramentalism of Christian orthodoxy, in which all natural things are symbols and images of the divine transcendence, but in which the tension between the present and the future of prophetic religion is destroyed, is a priestly deflation of prophetic religion. In genuinely prophetic religion the God who transcends the created world also convicts a sinful world of its iniquities and promises an ultimate redemption from them. The realm of redemption is never, as in rational and mystical religion, above the realm of living history, but within and at the end of it. The insistence of the Hebrew upon the sacred meaning of this life (the soul resides significantly in the blood in Hebrew mythology) is the root of all modern naturalisms, liberal and radical; though in the original Hebraic mythical view the processes of nature and history are never self-sufficient, self-explanatory, and self-redeeming. God will redeem history (that is the mythical emphasis in contrast to naturalism) but it is the living world in its history which will be redeemed (that is the mythical emphasis in contrast to the other-worldliness of rational-mystical religion).

The prophetic movement in Hebraic religion offers an interesting confirmation of the thesis that a genuine faith in transcendence is the power which lifts religion above its culture and emancipates it from sharing the fate of dying cultures. The prophets saved Hebraic religion from extinction when the Babylonian exile ended the Hebraic culture-religion with its centre in the worship of the Temple. They not only saved the life of religion, but raised it to a new purity by their interpretation of the meaning of catastrophe, the redemptive power of vicarious suffering, and the possibility of a redemption which would include more than the fortunes of Israel. In somewhat the same fashion Augustine's faith disassociated Christianity from a dying Roman world, though the Greek other-worldly elements in Augustine's faith created the basis for a sacramental rather than prophetic religion of transcendence. Catholic orthodoxy survived the Graeco-Roman culture in the matrix of which it was formed, but in it Isaiah's hope for redemption at the end of history was replaced by a reference toward a realm of transcendence above history, between which and the world of nature-history a sacramental institution mediated. Thus Catholic orthodoxy robbed prophetic religion of its interest in future history and destroyed the sense of the dynamic character of mundane existence.

A vital, prophetic Christianity is consequently forced not only to maintain its independence against naturalism and other-worldliness, but to preserve its purity against sacramental vitiations of its own basic prophetic mythology. The inclination of Christianity to deviate from prophetic religion in terms of sacramental complacency on the one hand and mystic other-worldliness on the other is partly derived from the Greek influence upon its thought and is partly the consequence of its own commendable sharpening of the religious tension in prophetic religion. The religion of Jesus is prophetic religion in which the moral ideal of love and vicarious suffering, elaborated by the second Isaiah, achieves such a purity that the possibility of its realization in history becomes remote. His Kingdom of God is always a possibility in history, because its heights of pure love are organically related to the experience of love in all human life, but it is also an impossibility in history and always beyond every historical achievement. Men living in nature and in the body will never be capable of the sublimation of egoism and the attainment of the sacrificial passion, the complete disinterestedness which the ethic of Jesus demands. The social justice which Amos demanded represented a possible ideal for society. Jesus' conception of pure love is related to the idea of justice as the holiness of God is related to the goodness of men. It transcends the possible and historical. Perhaps this is the reason why the eschatology of later prophecy had ceased to be as unambiguously this-worldly as was that of early prophecy. Certainly the eschatology of Jesus, though this-worldly in framework, went beyond the possibilities of natural existence ("In the Kingdom of God there will be neither marrying nor giving in marriage"). It might not be unfair to suggest, therefore, that in Christianity the tension between the possibilities of nature and the religio-moral ideal is heightened to a degree which imperils the sober this-worldliness of Hebrew religion. Perhaps the influence of Greek mystery religions upon Christian thought was only a final weight in the balance on the side of dualism, rather than its chief source. This final weight was exerted as early as the thought of Paul ("flesh and blood cannot inherit the Kingdom of God, neither can corruption inherit incorruption") and continues to increase in the theological elaboration of Christian faith by the early Fathers. The mythical basis of Christian thought prevented it from ever falling into the worst vices of rationalistic dualism, witness the victorious conflict of Christian orthodoxy against Manichaeism and Gnosticism. But it was natural that the highly refined prophetic tensions of the original gospel should become relaxed under the pressure of the years and the effect of rough history upon its delicate resiliency. The consequence of this relaxation is seen in the sacramentalism of Christian orthodoxy in which the natural world (including, unfortunately, the social orders of human history) is celebrated as the handiwork of God; and every natural fact is rightly seen as an image of the transcendent, but wrongly covered so completely with the aura of sanctity as to obscure its imperfections. This sacramentalism is a constitutional disease of mythical religion. The pessimism, asceticism, and mystical absorption which have occasionally seeped into Christian thought and life are not native to it, but derive from rationalistic and mystical religions. Naturalism is another aberration native rather than foreign to the Christian-Hebrew mythos. It maintains the Hebraic idea of the dynamic character of history, but empties its world of references to the transcendent source of life and meaning, thus arriving at its self-contained and self-sufficient history. If sacramentalism destroys the horizontal tension between present and future, naturalism vitiates the vertical tension between concrete fact and transcendent source.

A vital Christian faith and life is thus under the necessity of perennially preserving its health against the peril of diseases and corruptions arising out of its own life; and of protecting itself against errors to which non-mythical religions tempt it. Most of its own weaknesses arise when the mythical paradoxes of its faith are resolved; most of the perils from the outside come from the pessimism and dualism of mystical and rational religion. Only a vital Christian faith, renewing its youth in its prophetic origin, is capable of dealing adequately with the moral and social problems of our age; only such a faith can affirm the significance of temporal and mundane existence without capitulating unduly to the relativities of the temporal process. Such a faith alone can point to a source of meaning which transcends all the little universes of value and meaning which "have their day and cease to be" and yet not seek refuge in an eternal world where all history ceases to be significant. Only such a faith can outlast the death of old cultures and the birth of new civilizations, and yet deal in terms of moral responsibility with the world in which cultures and civilizations engage in struggles of death and life.

2

THE ETHIC OF JESUS

The ethic of Jesus is the perfect fruit of prophetic religion. Its
ideal of love has the same relation to the facts and necessities of
human experience as the God of prophetic faith has to the world.
It is drawn from, and relevant to, every moral experience. It is
immanent in life as God is immanent in the world. It transcends
the possibilities of human life in its final pinnacle as God
transcends the world. It must, therefore, be confused neither with
the ascetic ethic of world-denying religions nor with the prudential morality of naturalism, designed to guide good people to
success and happiness in this world. It is easily confused with the
former because of its uncompromising attitude toward all the
impulses of nature; but it never condemns natural impulse as
inherently bad. It may be confused with the latter because the
transcendent character of its love ideal is implicit rather than
explicit in the teachings of Jesus. The ethic proceeds logically
from the presuppositions of prophetic religion. In prophetic
religion God, as creator and judge of the world, is both the unity
which is the ground of existence and the ultimate unity, the good
which is, to use Plato's phrase, on the other side of existence. In as
far as the world exists at all it is good; for existence is possible only
when chaos is overcome by unity and order. But the unity of the
world is threatened by chaos, and its meaningfulness is always
under the peril of meaninglessness. The ultimate confidence in the
meaningfulness of life, therefore, rests upon a faith in the final

unity, which transcends the world's chaos as certainly as it is basic to the world's order.

The unity of God is not static, but potent and creative. God is, therefore, love. The conscious impulse of unity between life and life is the most adequate symbol of his nature. All life stands under responsibility to this loving will. In one sense the ethic which results from the command of love is related to any possible ethical system; for all moral demands are demands of unity. Life must not be lived at cross-purposes. The self must establish an inner unity of impulses and desires and it must relate itself harmoniously to other selves and other unities. Thus Hobhouse correctly defines the good as "harmony in the fulfilment of vital capacity."[1] But every naturalistic ethic can demand no more than harmony within chaos, love within the possibilities set by human egoism. A prudential ethic, seeking to relate life to life on the level of nature, is either based upon the illusion that a basic natural harmony between life exists (either because egoism supposedly balances egoism in harmless reciprocity or because rational egoism overcomes conflicts on lower levels of less rational impulse), or it is forced to give sanction to the conflict of egoistic individuals and groups as of the very essence of human character. It is in its attitude toward the force of egoism that the ethic of Jesus distinguishes itself from every naturalistic and prudential ethic. Egoism is not regarded as harmless because imbedded in a pre-established harmony (Adam Smith), nor as impotent because reason can transmute its anarchies into a higher harmony (utilitarianism), nor as the basic reality of human existence (Thomas Hobbes).

The ethic of Jesus does not deal at all with the immediate moral problem of every human life—the problem of arranging some kind of armistice between various contending factions and forces. It has nothing to say about the relativities of politics and economics, nor of the necessary balances of power which exist and must exist in even the most intimate social relationships. The absolutism and perfectionism of Jesus' love ethic sets itself uncompromisingly not only against the natural self-regarding

---

[1] L. T. Hobhouse, *The Rational Good*, p. 161.

impulses, but against the necessary prudent defences of the self, required because of the egoism of others. It does not establish a connection with the horizontal points of a political or social ethic or with the diagonals which a prudential individual ethic draws between the moral ideal and the facts of a given situation. It has only a vertical dimension between the loving will of God and the will of man.

Love as the quintessence of the character of God is not established by argument, but taken for granted. It may be regarded as axiomatic in the faith of prophetic religion. On the only occasion on which Jesus makes the matter a subject for argument he declares: "If ye then, being evil, know how to give good gifts unto your children, how much more shall your Father which is in heaven give good things to them that ask him?"[1] This passage is significant because Jesus, true to the insights of prophetic religion, not only discovers symbols of the character of God in man's mundane existence, in the tenderness of parents toward their children, but also because he sees this symbol of God's love among "evil" and not among imperfect men. The contrast in prophetic religion is not between perfection and imperfection, or between the temporal and the eternal, but between good and evil will. But since the evil will of man is not the consequence of pure finiteness, the life of man is not without symbols and echoes of the divine.

In another significant passage the impartiality of nature is made the symbol of divine grace. Since God permits the sun to shine upon the evil and the good and sends the rain upon the just and the unjust, we are to love our enemies.[2] The argument used is important not only because an infra-moral aspect of nature is used as a symbol of the supra-moral character of divine grace (thus expressing prophetic imagination at its best), but also because emulation of the character of God is advanced as the only motive of forgiving enemies. Nothing is said about the possibility of transmuting their enmity to friendship through the practice of forgiveness. That social and prudential possibility has been read into the admonition of Jesus by liberal Christianity.

---

[1] Matt. vii. 11.
[2] Matt. v. 45.

The rigorism of the gospel ethic and its failure to make concessions to even the most inevitable and "natural" self-regarding impulses may best be judged by analysing the attitude of Jesus toward various natural expressions of human life. Every form of self-assertion is scrutinized and condemned in words which allow of no misinterpretation.

The very basis of self-love is the natural will to survive. In man the animal impulse to maintain life becomes an immediate temptation to assert the self against the neighbour. Therefore, in the ethic of Jesus, concern for physical existence is prohibited: "Take no thought for your life, what ye shall eat, or what ye shall drink; nor yet for your body, what ye shall put on. Is not the life more than meat and the body more than raiment? Behold the fowls of the air: for they sow not, neither do they reap, nor gather into barns; yet your heavenly Father feedeth them. Are ye not much better than they? . . . Therefore take no thought, saying, What shall we eat? or, What shall we drink? or, Wherewithal shall we be clothed? For after all these things do the Gentiles seek; for your heavenly Father knoweth that ye have need of all these things."[1] The prudent conscience will have an immediately unfavourable reaction to these words. No life can be lived in such unconcern for the physical basis of life. Those who try to make the ethic of Jesus a guide to prudent conduct have, therefore, been anxious to point out that the naïve faith in God's providential care which underlies these injunctions had more relevance in the simple agrarian life of Palestine than in the economic complexities of modern urban existence. But it must be noted that they cannot be followed absolutely even in simple agrarian life. The fact is that this word contains a completely unprudential rigorism in the ethic of Jesus which appears again and again.

The most natural expansion of the self is the expansion through possessions. Therefore the love of possessions as a form of self-assertion meets the same uncompromising rigour. "Lay not up for yourselves treasures upon earth . . . for where your treasure is, there will your heart be also. . . . No man can serve two masters. . . . Ye cannot serve God and mammon."[2] Here the

---

[1] Matt. vi. 25-32.
[2] Matt. vi. 19-24.

religious orientation of the ethic is perfectly clear. Love of possession is a distraction which makes love and obedience to God impossible. God demands absolute obedience. Thus the rich young ruler who has kept all the commandments is advised, "Go and sell that thou hast, and give to the poor."[1] This word has been used to establish a basis for an ascetic ethic, but it probably was not meant as a rule in the thought of Jesus. It was meant rather as a test of complete devotion to the sovereignty of God. In the same manner the poor widow is praised above those who gave of their superfluity because she "gave all she had"[2] Somewhat in the same category is the parable of the great supper from which some of the guests excluded themselves because of their preoccupation with the land or the oxen they had bought and the wife one had married.[3] In all these instances the attitude toward wealth is not determined by any socio-moral considerations, but rather by the conviction that wealth is a source of distraction. The key to Jesus' attitude on wealth is most succinctly stated in the words, "Where your treasure is there will your heart be also."

The most penetrating analyses of the character of self-love are to be found in Jesus' excoriation of pride, particularly the pride of good people. Pride is a subtle form of self-love. It feeds not on the material advantages which more greedy people seek, but upon social approval. His strictures against the Pharisees were partly directed against their social pride. "All their works they do for to be seen of men . . . and love the uppermost rooms at feasts and the chief seats in the synagogues and greetings in the markets and to be called of men, Rabbi, Rabbi."[4] In the same spirit is the advice to dinner guests, at the house of one of the chief Pharisees "when he marked how they chose out the chief rooms." . . . "But when thou art bidden, go and sit down in the lowest room. . . . For whosoever exalteth himself shall be abased: and he that humbleth himself shall be exalted."[5] Incidentally in this case the subjection of egoistic pride is justified not only in religious terms, but in terms of prudential morality. It is pointed out that the effort of the proud to reach exalted positions in society actually results in a

---

[1] Matt. xix. 21.
[2] Mark xii. 44.
[3] Luke xiv. 16-24.
[4] Matt. xxiii. 5-7.
[5] Luke xiv. 7-11.

loss of respect, while humility leads to social approval: "When he that bade thee cometh, he may say unto thee, Friend, go up higher: then shalt thou have worship in the presence of them that sit at meat with thee."[1] This note of prudence is somewhat at variance with the general more purely religious orientation of Jesus' ethic. The same emphasis is found in the words "Whosoever will be great among you, shall be your minister: and whosoever of you will be the chiefest, shall be the servant of all."[2] Pride is the form of egoism which corrupts the spirits of all those who possess some excellency of knowledge or achievement which distinguishes them from the crowd, so that they forget their common humanity and their equal unworthiness in the sight of God. But the spiritual pride and self-righteousness which fails to detect the alloy of sin in the relative virtues achieved according to moral codes belongs in yet another category and must be dealt with separately.

Jesus' attitude toward vindictiveness and his injunction to forgive the enemy reveals more clearly than any other element in his ethic his intransigence against forms of self-assertion which have social and moral approval in any natural morality. Resentment against injustice is both the basis, and the egoistic corruption of, all forms of corrective justice. Every communal punishment of murder is a refinement of early customs of blood vengeance. The early community permitted and even encouraged blood vengeance because it felt that the destruction of life within the community was wrong; but it left punishment in the hands of a blood relative because the vindictive passion of the injured family was more potent than the community's more dispassionate disapproval of murder. From the first restraints upon blood vengeance to the last refinements of corrective justice, the egoistic element of vindictiveness remains both an inevitable and a dangerous alloy in the passion for justice. It is inevitable because men never judge injustice so severly as it ought to be judged until their life, or life in their intimate circle, is destroyed by it. It is dangerous because, informed not by a passion for all life, but by attachment to a particular life, it may, and frequently does, do as much injury to

---

[1] Luke xiv. 10.
[2] Mark x. 43.

life as it seeks to correct. But it remains inevitable however dangerous it may be. Self-assertion when the self is in peril or the victim of injustice expresses itself as a natural impulse even in persons who know its dangers and disapprove the logic which underlies it.

Neither its inevitability nor its moral or social justification in immediate situations qualifies the rigour of Jesus' position. Men are enjoined to "love their enemies," to "forgive, not seven times, but seventy times seven," to resist evil, to turn the other cheek, to go the second mile, to bless them that curse you and do good to them that hate you. In all these injunctions both resistance and resentment are forbidden. The self is not to assert its interests against those who encroach upon it, and not to resent the injustice done to it. The modern pulpit would be saved from much sentimentality if the thousands of sermons which are annually preached upon these texts would contain some suggestions of the impossibility of these ethical demands for natural man in his immediate situations. Nowhere is the ethic of Jesus in more obvious conflict with both the impulses and the necessities of ordinary men in typical social situations.

The justification for these demands is put in purely religious and not in socio-moral terms. We are to forgive because God forgives;[1] we are to love our enemies because God is impartial in his love. The points of reference are vertical and not horizontal. Neither natural impulses nor social consequences are taken into consideration. It is always possible, of course, that absolute ethical attitudes have desirable social consequences. To do good to an enemy may prompt him to overcome his enmity; and forgiveness of evil may be a method of redemption which commends itself to the most prudent. It must be observed, however, that no appeal to social consequences could ever fully justify these demands of Jesus. Non-resistance may shame an aggressor into goodness, but it may also prompt him to further aggression. Furthermore, if the action is motivated by regard for social consequences it will hardly be pure enough to secure the consequences which are supposed to justify it. Upon that paradox all purely prudential morality is shattered. Therefore Jesus ad-

---

[1] Matt. xviii. 23.

monishes the disciples who rejoice that "the devils are subject unto us in thy name" not to rejoice in success—"rejoice not that the devils are subject unto you, but rather rejoice because your names are written in heaven."[1] One might paraphrase that injunction as follows: Find your satisfaction not in the triumph over evil in existence, but rather in the conformity of your life to its ultimate essence. Jesus' attitude toward the woman taken in adultery and his confounding word to the self-righteous judges, "Let him who is without sin cast the first stone," shows the relation of his idea of contrition to that of forgiveness. We are to forgive those who wrong society not only because God forgives, but because we know that in the sight of God we also are sinners. This insight into, and emphasis upon, the sins of the righteous is derived from the religious perspective; but it has a very practical relevance to the problems of society. The society which punishes criminals is never so conscious as it might be of the degree to which it is tainted with, and responsible for, the very sins which it abhors and punishes. Yet an unqualified insistence upon guiltlessness as a prerequisite of the right to punish would invalidate every measure required for the maintenance of social order. It is, therefore, impossible to construct a socio-moral policy from this religio-moral insight of Jesus', as, for instance, Tolstoi attempted in his objection to jails and other forms of social punishment. Society must punish criminals, or at least quarantine them, even if the executors of judgment are self-righteous sinners who do not realize to what degree they are involved in the sins they seek to suppress. But this fact does not invalidate the insight which sees the relative good and the relative evil in both judges and criminals from a high perspective.

The effort to elaborate the religio-moral thought of Jesus into a practical socio-moral or even politico-moral system usually has the effect of blunting the very penetration of his moral insights. When, for instance, liberal Christianity defines the doctrine of non-resistance, so that it becomes merely an injunction against violence in conflict, it ceases to provide a perspective from which the sinful element in all resistance, conflict, and coercion may be discovered. Its application prompts moral complacency rather

---

[1] Luke x. 20.

than contrition, and precisely in those groups in which the evils
which flow from self-assertion are most covert. This is the pathos
of the espousal of Christian pacifism by the liberal Church,
ministering largely to those social groups who have the economic
power to be able to dispense with the more violent forms of
coercion and therefore condemn them as un-Christian.

The love absolutism in the ethic of Jesus expresses itself in
terms of a universalism, set against all narrower forms of human
sympathy, as well as in terms of a perfectionism which maintains a
critical vigour against the most inevitable and subtle forms of
self-assertion. The universalistic element appears in the injunctions which require that the life of the neighbour be affirmed
beyond the bounds set by natural human sympathy. Love within
the bounds of consanguinity and intimate community is regarded
as devoid of special merit: "For if ye love them which love you,
what thanks have ye? Do not even the publicans the same?"[1] An
all-embracing love is enjoined because God's love is like that. In
Professor Torrey's recent translation of the four gospels, Matt.
v. 48 is rendered in words which fit in perfectly with the general
logic of Jesus' thought: "Be therefore all-including in your good-
will, as your Heavenly Father includes all."[2]

The universalism in Jesus' ethic has affinities with Stoic
universalism, but there are also important differences between
them. In Stoicism life beyond the narrow bonds of class, community, and race is to be affirmed because all life reveals a unifying,
divine principle. Since the divine principle is reason, the logic of
Stoicism tends to include only the intelligent in the divine
community. An aristocratic condescension, therefore, corrupts
Stoic universalism. In the thought of Jesus men are to be loved not
because they are equally divine, but because God loves them
equally; and they are to be forgiven (the highest form of love)
because all (the self included) are equally far from God and in need
of his grace. This difference between Stoicism and the gospel
ethic is important because it marks a real distinction between
pantheism and prophetic religion. The ultimate moral demands
upon man can never be affirmed in terms of the actual facts of

---

[1] Matt. v. 46.
[2] Charles Cutler Torrey, *The Four Gospels*, p. 12.

human existence. They can be affirmed only in terms of a unity and a possibility, a divine reality which transcends human existence. The order of human existence is too imperilled by chaos, the goodness of man too corrupted by sin, and the possibilities of man too obscured by natural handicaps to make human order and human virtue and human possibilities solid bases of the moral imperative.

The universalistic note in the thought of Jesus is reinforced by his critical attitude toward the family. This attitude is particularly significant because he was not an ascetic in his family ethic. On the contrary, he had a sacramental conception of the family relation. Yet family loyalty is seen as a possible hindrance to a higher loyalty. When appraised of the presence of the members of his family he answers ruthlessly: "Who is my mother, or my brethren? . . . For whosoever shall do the will of God, the same is my brother, and my sister, and mother."[1] In the same spirit is his advice to the young man who desired to withhold his discipleship until he could perform the last act of filial piety, "Let the dead bury the dead"[2]; and also the uncompromising words "He that loveth father or mother more than me is not worthy of me"[3] (given an even more ruthless form in Luke xiv. 26, "If any man come to me, and hate not his father, and mother, and wife, and children, and brethren, and sisters, yea, and his own life also, he cannot be my disciple"). Surely this is not an ethic which can give us specific guidance in the detailed problems of social morality where the relative claims of family, community, class, and nation must be constantly weighed. One is almost inclined to agree with Karl Barth that this ethic "is not applicable to the problems of contemporary society nor yet to any conceivable society." It is oriented by only one vertical religious reference, to the will of God; and the will of God is defined in terms of all-inclusive love. Under the perspective of that will the realities of the world of human egoism, and the injustices and tyrannies arising from it, are fully revealed. We see the actual facts more clearly and realize that the world of nature is also a world of sin. But there is no advice

---

[1] Mark iii. 32-34.
[2] Luke ix. 60.
[3] Matt. x. 37.

on how we may hold the world of sin in check until the coming of the Kingdom of God. The ethic of Jesus may offer valuable insights to and sources of criticism for a prudential social ethic which deals with present realities; but no such social ethic can be directly derived from a pure religious ethic.

If there are any doubts about the predominant vertical religious reference of Jesus' ethic they ought to be completely laid by a consideration of his attitude on the ethical problem of rewards. Here the full rigorism and the non-prudential character of Jesus' ethic are completely revealed. Obedience to God, in the teachings of Jesus, must be absolute and must not be swayed by any ulterior considerations. Alms are not to be done before men and prayers are not to be said in the market place, so that the temptation to gain social approval through religious piety and good works may be overcome.[1] Good deeds from which mutual advantages may be secured are to be eschewed: "But when thou makest a meal, call the poor, the maimed, the lame, the blind, and thou shalt be blessed; for they cannot recompense thee."[2] The service of God is to be performed not only without hope of any concrete or obvious reward, but at the price of sacrifice, abnegation, and loss. "He that taketh not his cross, and followeth after me, is not worthy of me."[3] The sovereignty of God is pictured as a pearl of great price or like a treasure hid in a field which to buy men sell all they have.[4] If any natural gift or privilege should become a hindrance to the spirit of perfect obedience to God it must be rigorously denied: "If thine eye offend thee, pluck it out, and cast it from thee: it is better for thee to enter into life with one eye, rather than, having two eyes, to be cast into hell fire."[5] In all of these emphases the immediate and the concrete advantages which may flow from right conduct are either not considered at all or their consideration is definitely excluded. The ethic demands an absolute obedience to the will of God without consideration of those consequences of moral action which must be the concern of any prudential ethic.

It must be admitted that this rigour is seemingly qualified by certain promises of reward. These rewards belong in two

---

[1] Matt. vi. 1-6.
[2] Luke xiv. 13-15.
[3] Matt. x. 38.
[4] Matt. xiii. 44-46.
[5] Matt. xviii. 9.

categories. The one is ultimate rewards "in the resurrection of the just." The others are probably a concession to a prudential morality. The merciful shall obtain mercy (does this mean from God or from man?). Men will be measured by the measure with which they mete and if they do not judge they will not be judged (Matt. vii. 1). This may mean that God will deal with men according to their attitude toward their fellow-men (a considera-tion suggested in the parable of the last judgment); but it may also mean that Jesus is calling attention to the reciprocal character of all social life where censoriousness is met by a critical attitude, and where pride actually results in the disrespect of one's fellows, while humility elicits respect: ("whosoever exalteth himself shall be abased; and he that humbleth himself shall be exalted").[1] In the same category is the ethical paradox which is so basic to the ethics of Jesus: "He that findeth his life shall lose it: and he that loseth his life for my sake, shall find it."[2] This paradox merely calls attention to the fact that egoism is self-defeating, while self-sacrifice actually leads to a higher form of self-realization. Thus self-love is never justified, but self-realization is allowed as the unintended but inevitable consequence of unselfish action.

This note in the teachings of Jesus brings it into a position of relevance with a social and prudential ethic. It has even estab-lished points of contact between the ethic of Jesus and a utilitarian ethic in which the conflict between love and self-love is sup-posedly resolved by the achievement of a form of selfishness which includes "the greatest good of the greatest number." It must be remembered, however, that the actual world of human nature and history does not by any means guarantee self-realization through self-sacrifice unless self-realization is conceived in terms quite distinct from the ordinary will-to-survive in physical life. History may bestow immortality of fame upon a martyr, but it certainly does not guarantee that an honest man will prosper because of his honesty or an unselfish man succeed because of his generosity. There are always such possibilities in the world because the human world contains symbols of ultimate unity amidst its chaos. But it is not a world of pure unity and the

---

[1] Luke xiv. 11.
[2] Matt. x. 39.

imperative of love leads to the destruction of the self as well as to its higher fulfilment.

Possibly Jesus thought of all these rewards only in eschatological terms. He may have meant to say only that God would be merciful to the merciful, would exalt the humble, and would establish the life of those who had lost it for the Kingdom's sake. Most of the promises of reward in the teachings of Jesus are clearly in this category of ultimate rewards. Those who have left house and family are promised "manifold more in this present time, and in the world to come life everlasting."[1] In the parable of the talents the obedient servant is set in "authority over ten cities."[2] Those who are reviled are given the promise and hope of a great reward in heaven.[3] The rich young man is promised "treasure in heaven" if his obedience is complete enough to prompt him to sell all he has.[4]

All these promises of an ultimate reward are in no way in conflict with the rigour of the gospel ethic. They merely prove that even the most uncompromising ethical system must base its moral imperative on an order of reality and not merely on a possibility. Somewhere, somehow, the unity of the world must be or become an established fact and not merely a possibility, and actions which flow from its demands must be in harmony and not in conflict with reality. Such assurances may always become the basis of a "transcendental hedonism" and persuade the faithful to seek ultimate rewards by courting momentary loss. But this attitude toward ultimate rewards does not discredit a religion which promises them. It merely proves that human egoism can corrupt even the most ultimate hopes and make them the basis of self-seeking. It is as pathetic as it is natural that human sin should express itself finally in an effort to corrupt the ultimate hope of the human spirit.

The eschatological character of the promise of rewards in the gospel ethic naturally raises the question of the relation of this ethic to eschatology. If by an eschatological ethic is meant an "interims" ethic, an ethic to be followed in the short period before the coming of the Kingdom of God, an ethic which regards the

---

[1] Luke xviii. 30.
[2] Luke xix. 17.
[3] Matt. v. 11.
[4] Luke xviii. 22.

affairs of this world with indifference and contempt because the end of the world is imminent, the ethic of Jesus is definitely not in this category. The note of apocalyptic urgency is significantly lacking in many of the passages in which the religio-ethical rigour is most uncompromising.[1] The motive advanced for fulfilling the absolute demands is simply that of obedience to God or emulation of his nature, and there is no suggestion that the world should be held in contempt because it will soon pass away. In St Paul the interims motif is more pronounced, particularly in his family ethic.[2] Confidence in the imminent destruction of the present world order prompts him to counsel indifference toward relationships the significance of which depends upon its continuance. Jesus' attitude toward the family is entirely different. It is, on the whole, sacramental ("what God hath joined let no man put asunder"). Where it approaches the ascetic, as, for instance, in the identification of lust with adultery, the rigorous note has no relation to the apocalyptic element. It is merely a consistent part of the entire emphasis upon absolute purity of motive in the total system of thought.

There is, nevertheless, an eschatological element in, and even basis for, the ethic of Jesus. The ethical demands made by Jesus are incapable of fulfilment in the present existence of man. They proceed from a transcendent and divine unity of essential reality, and their final fulfilment is possible only when God transmutes the present chaos of this world into its final unity. The logic of this thought is obviously under the influence of the later apocalypses of Jewish prophecy in which the hope for a "good time" and a "fulfilled time" becomes transmuted into the expectation of the end of time. These later apocalypses were the consequence of a logic inherent in the moral life, a logic which recognizes that the ultimate moral demands upon the human spirit proceed from a unity which transcends all conceivable possibilities in the order of nature and history in which human life moves. Placing the final fulfilment at the end of time and not in a realm above temporality is to remain true to the genius of prophetic religion and to state mythically what cannot be stated rationally. If stated rationally

---

[1] *Cf.* Matt. v. 29; vi. 20, 31; x. 37; xii. 48; Luke xviii. 22.
[2] 1 Cor. vii. 27-29.

the world is divided between the temporal and the eternal and only the eternal forms above the flux of temporality have significance. To state the matter mythically is to do justice to the fact that the eternal can only be fulfilled in the temporal. But since myth is forced to state a paradoxical aspect of reality in terms of concepts connoting historical sequence, it always leads to historical illusions. Jesus, no less than Paul, was not free of these historical illusions. He expected the coming of the Messianic kingdom in his lifetime; at least that seems to have been his expectation before the crisis in his ministry. Even when he faced the cross rather than triumph he merely postponed the ultimate triumph to a later future, though to a rather proximate one.[1]

Apocalypticism in terms of a specific interpretation of history may thus be regarded as the consequence and not the cause of Jesus' religion and ethic. The apocalypse is a mythical expression of the impossible possibility under which all human life stands. The Kingdom of God is always at hand in the sense that the impossibilities are really possible, and lead to new actualities in given moments of history. Nevertheless every actuality of history reveals itself, after the event, as only an approximation of the ideal; and the Kingdom of God is therefore not here. It is in fact always coming but never here.

The historical illusions which resulted inevitably from this mythical statement of the situation in which the human spirit finds itself do not destroy the truth in the myth; no more than the discovery that the fall of man was not actual history destroys the mythical truth in the story of the fall. Nevertheless it must be admitted that the ethical rigour of the early Church was maintained through the hope of the second coming of Christ and the establishment of his Kingdom. When the hope of the *parousia* waned the rigour of the Christian ethic was gradually dissipated and the Church, forced to come to terms with the relativities of politics and economics and the immediate necessities of life, made unnecessary compromises with these relativities which frequently imperilled the very genius of prophetic religion. But the mistakes which resulted, both from illusions about the course of history

---

[1] *Cf.* Matt. x. 23. "Ye shall not have gone through the cities of Israel, until the Son of man be come."

and from the adjustments which had to be made when the illusions vanished, do not invalidate the basic insights of prophetic religion. They merely present Christian ethics afresh with the problem of compromise, the problem of creating and maintaining tentative harmonies of life in the world in terms of the possibilities of the human situation, while yet at the same time preserving the indictment upon all human life of the impossible possibility, the law of love.

As I understand it, the two Rauschenbush lectures previous to this one took opposite views on the so-called apostasy of the Church after Constantine from the ethic of Jesus. In one[1] it was maintained that the rigour of the early Church should have been maintained and must at all costs be re-established. This thesis does not recognize to what degree the particular ethical strategy of the early Church depended upon an illusion in regard to history. In the other[2] the compromises of the Church are interpreted as merely necessary adaptations of the Christian conscience to new situations. Dr. Case declares: "There is a wide range of social tasks that were but dimly, if at all, perceived in ancient times. However loyal the individual may be to the Christian heritage, he frequently finds it deficient as a guide to all his conduct when he is faced with the more crucial issues of the present. Even the problems of personal conduct have taken on many new aspects in the history of social evolution since the time of Jesus."[3] The unique rigour of the gospel ethic is thus attributed to the peculiar circumstances of time and place—agrarian simplicity, for instance, as contrasted with the industrial complexities of our own day. Both interpretations flow from the same illusion of liberalism, that we are dealing with a possible and prudential ethic in the gospel. In the one case its unqualified application is recommended in spite of the fact that every moment of our existence reveals its impossibility. In the other case, necessary compromises are regarded merely as adjustments to varying ages and changing circumstances. The crucial problem of Christian ethics is obscured in either case.

The full dimension of human life includes not only an impossi-

---

[1] Charles Clayton Morrison, *The Social Gospel and the Christian Cultus*, chap. vi.
[2] Shirley Jackson Case, *The Social Triumph of the Ancient Church*.
[3] *Op. cit.*, p. 12.

ble ideal, but realities of sin and evil which are more than simple imperfections and which prove that the ideal is something more than the product of a morbidly sensitive religious fantasy. Anything less than perfect love in human life is destructive of life. All human life stands under an impending doom because it does not live by the law of love. Egoism is always destructive. The wages of sin is death. The destruction of our contemporary civilization through its injustice and through the clash of conflicting national wills is merely one aspect and one expression of the destruction of sin in the world.

Confronted with this situation humanity always faces a double task. The one is to reduce the anarchy of the world to some kind of immediately sufferable order and unity; and the other is to set these tentative and insecure unities and achievements under the criticism of the ultimate ideal. When they are not thus challenged, what is good in them becomes evil and each tentative harmony becomes the cause of a new anarchy. With Augustine we must realize that the peace of the world is gained by strife. That does not justify us either in rejecting such a tentative peace or in accepting it as final. The peace of the city of God can use and transmute the lesser and insecure peace of the city of the world; but that can be done only if the peace of the world is not confused with the ultimate peace of God.

3

THE CHRISTIAN
CONCEPTION OF SIN

The measure of Christianity's success in gauging the full dimension of human life is given in its love perfectionism, on the one hand, and in its moral realism and pessimism, on the other. In liberal Christianity there is an implicit assumption that human nature has the resources to fulfil what the gospel demands. The Kantian axiom, "I ought, therefore I can," is accepted as basic to all analyses of the moral situation. In classical Christianity the perfectionism of the gospel stands in a much more difficult relation to the estimate of human resources. The love commandment stands in juxtaposition to the fact of sin. It helps, in fact, to create the consciousness of sin. When, as in utilitarian doctrine, the moral ideal is stated in terms of a wise egoism, able to include the interests of others in those of the self, there is no occasion for the consciousness of sin. All human actions are simply on a lower or higher scale of rational adjustment of interest to interest and life to life.

The sense of sin is peculiarly the product of religious imagination, as the critics of religion quite rightly maintain. It is the consequence of measuring life in its total dimension and discovering the self both related to and separated from life in its essence. The consciousness of sin has no meaning to the mind of modernity because in modern secularism reality is merely a flux of temporal events. In prophetic religion the flux of the finite world is both a revelation and a veiling of the eternal creative principle and will.

Every finite event points to something beyond itself in two directions, to a source from which it springs and an end to which it moves. Prophetic religion believes, in other words, in a God who is both the creator and the fulfilment of life.

The human spirit is set in this dimension of depth in such a way that it is able to apprehend, but not to comprehend, the total dimension. The human mind is forced to relate all finite events to causes and consummations beyond themselves. It thus constantly conceives all particular things in their relation to the totality of reality, and can adequately apprehend totality only in terms of a principle of unity "beyond, behind, and above the passing flux of things" (Whitehead). But this same human reason is itself imbedded in the passing flux, a tool of a finite organism, the instrument of its physical necessities, and the prisoner of the partial perspectives of a limited time and place. The consequence is that it is always capable of envisaging possibilities of order, unity, and harmony above and beyond the contingent and arbitrary realities of its physical existence; but it is not capable (because of its finiteness) of incarnating all the higher values which it discerns, nor even of adequately defining the unconditioned good which it dimly apprehends as the ground and goal of all its contingent values.

This paradoxical relation of finitude and infinity, and consequently of freedom and necessity, is the mark of the uniqueness of the human spirit in this creaturely world. Man is the only mortal animal who knows that he is mortal, a fact which proves that in some sense he is not mortal. Man is the only creature imbedded in the flux of finitude who knows that this is his fate; which proves that in some sense this is not his fate. Thus when life is seen in its total dimension, the sense of God and the sense of sin are involved in the same act of self-consciousness; for to be self-conscious is to see the self as a finite object separated from essential reality; but also related to it, or there could be no knowledge of separation. If this religious feeling is translated into moral terms it becomes the tension between the principle of love and the impulse of egoism, between the obligation to affirm the ultimate unity of life and the urge to establish the ego against all competing forms of life. The Christian approach to the problem of sin is, however, not exhausted in the recognition of mere finiteness. That recognition is in some sense involved in all moral and philosophical theory. All modern moral theory may be briefly described as complacent finiteness. The motto of modernity is succinctly given in the words of that typical spirit of the Renaissance, Cosimo de' Medici: "You follow infinite objects, I finite ones. You place your ladders in the heavens and I on earth that I may not seek so high or fall so low." The more classical culture religions, such as Neo-Platonism and Buddhism, are characterized by a tragic sense of finitude in which sin and evil are identified with temporality; and salvation is conceived as an escape from the temporal to the eternal world, an escape which necessarily involves the destruction of individual personality, since individuality is the product of finite existence. The conception of evil in prophetic religion is more complex than either of these.

Unlike modern secularism prophetic religion does not accept finitude complacently, for it recognizes that reality is more than flux. If it were not more than that there could be no meaningful existence; for the flux of the world is full of evil and every higher principle of order to which the soul might attach itself, in the effort to rescue meaning from chaos, is discovered, upon analysis, to have new possibilities of evil in it. The high values of history may be some tentative unity, like that of the nation, not high or inclusive enough to become the ultimate principle of order, and therefore a possible source of a new anarchy; or they may be a more ultimate conception of order like that of the community of mankind, which is corrupted as soon as it is incarnated, since the instruments of its realization are always specific men, groups, and nations, who are bound to introduce their partial perspectives and imperial lusts into the dream of the ideal.

While one must have considerable sympathy with modernity when it declaims with Cosimo de' Medici, "We will not aim so high or fall so low" when one surveys the havoc wrought by morbid religion, yet this sympathy is dissipated when it is recognized that it is not within the province of the human spirit to choose qualified goals in order to escape the intolerable tension of the unqualified. Every such effort merely results in transmuting some qualified end (such as democracy, the League of Nations, honesty in business, liberty, etc.) into an unqualified one. Man as a creature of both finitude and the eternal cannot escape his problem simply by disavowing the ultimate. The eternal is involved in every moral judgment. The moral theories of modern culture will be found, upon close examination, to deal with the unconditioned implicitly while they deny its validity explicitly. Does not all modern moral theory proceed upon the assumption that human reason will be able to arrive at higher and higher standards of impartial judgment and harmonies of conduct? While ostensibly glorying in the finitude of man, it really gives itself to the uncritical faith that human reason is slowly approaching a state of discarnate perfection; and that an adequate education will ultimately allow men to judge issues between themselves and their neighbours, as if their judgments were not always conditioned by the partial perspectives of a finite creature and corrupted by the will-to-live of natural man.

If modern naturalism ostensibly disavows the transcendent and unconditioned ground and fulfilment of the temporal flux while it really hopes for its realization in history, the more classical forms of non-mythical religion tend to identify sin with finiteness and salvation with escape from the flux of temporality. Modern naturalism is really a form of expansive pantheism, while the more rigorous types of rationalistic religion are contractive and result in an acosmic pantheism. In such pantheism the difference between good and evil is identical with the metaphysical distinction between the eternal and the temporal and between the spiritual and the material world. In the conception of such religion Santayana's judgment, that creation was really the fall, expresses the religious feeling precisely. The sense of sin is a sense of finiteness before the infinite, a feeling in which the metaphysical emphasis imperils the ethical connotation.

Both mysticism and asceticism are the natural fruits of such religious conceptions. In mysticism the effort is made to penetrate first to the rational and then to the ultra-rational essence of human existence in the confidence that man thus penetrates to the unconditioned essence of life, to God. The soul is thus conceived as a manifestation of God, encumbered in the evils of fleshly existence, but able to extricate itself by rational contemplation, mystic passivity, and intuition and ascetic discipline. "Only in so far as the soul is pure reason and pure contemplation is it free of the magic of nature," declared Plotinus. The path to eternity is thus the path from bodily impulse to reason and (since reason is itself a function of physical existence and has a divided and contingent world as its object) from reason to a super-rational contemplation of the unity of existence. This mystic contemplation is really the immediate awareness of the unity of consciousness; this unity being the symbol and the manifestation of the transcendent, the divine, and the eternal. "Sit in the centre of thyself and thou seest what is and shall be," declared a Sufi saint, and in a similar vein Catherine of Siena advised "If thou wouldst arrive at a perfect knowledge of Me the Eternal truth, never go outside thyself." From this emphasis upon the inner unity of consciousness as the real revelation of the eternal follows the mystic desire for passivity and the tendency toward asceticism. All natural interests are felt as distractions and all bodily functions and impulses as perils to the unity of the inner life. Of Plotinus, the founder of Neo-Platonism, his biographer wrote, "he seems to feel ashamed that his soul dwells in his body." Through ascetic discipline the soul hopes to free itself as much as possible from the cumbrous flesh. In Buddhism the various tendencies of these types of dualistic pantheism are driven to their logical conclusion and ultimate salvation is conceived as life in a state of quasi-existence, a state in which life and consciousness have been stripped of all that is finite, but also of all that is dynamic or meaningful.

A profound pathos thus hovers over the efforts of purely rational religions to deal with the problem of evil. In the modern naturalistic version of rational religion the tension between the eternal unity of existence and the evil of temporality is denied. In the more rigorous and classical versions of rationalistic religion the tension between the finite and the infinite, between the conditioned and unconditioned, is increased until the world breaks in two. Finite existence is left without meaning or significance, and eternity without content. The mind is separated from the body to preserve its purity, and thus it loses its individuality. The unity of consciousness loses reality by being falsely raised to the discarnate essence of reality.

The errors of these alternatives to prophetic religion must be understood if the true genius of a mythical approach to the

problem of sin and evil are to be understood. The genius of
prophetic Christianity's analysis of the facts of evil and sin are to
be found in the myth of the Fall. In this, as in every significant
myth of prophetic religion, the permanently valid insight must be
isolated from the primitive.

The particular virtue of the myth of the Fall is that it does
justice to the paradoxical relation of spirit and nature in human
evil. In the religious thought which flows from its interpretation
reason and consciousness are not the unqualified instruments of
good and the manifestations of the divine. Neither is the body or
material existence evil as such. Hence asceticism (with the
exception of certain forms of eschatological asceticism) is foreign
to prophetic religion. Where it exists in the Christian religion it
has usually been introduced by mystic influences essentially
foreign to the genius of prophetic religion. According to the myth
of the Fall, evil came into the world through human responsibility. It was neither ordained in the counsels of God nor the
inevitable consequence of temporal existence. Both the monistic
and dualistic pitfalls of consistent philosophy are thus avoided, at
the price, of course, of leaving the metaphysical problem at loose
ends. The origin of evil is attributed to an act of rebellion on the
part of man. Responsibility for the evil which threatens the unity
of existence is laid upon mankind, but this responsibility is
slightly qualified by the suggestion that man was tempted. The
serpent, symbol of the principle of evil, in the story of the Fall
does justice to the idea that human rebellion is not the first cause
and source of evil in the world. The world was not a perfect
harmony even before human sin created confusion. The idea in
Hebrew mythology that Satan is both a rebel against God and yet
ultimately under his dominion, expresses the paradoxical fact that
on the one hand evil is something more than the absence of order,
and on the other that it depends upon order. There can be disorder
only in an integrated world; and the forces of disorder can be
effective only if they are themselves ordered and integrated. Only
a highly cohesive nation can offer a threat to the peace of the
world. Thus the devil is possible only in a world controlled by
God and can be effective only if some of the potencies of the divine
are in him. Evil, in other words, is not the absence but the

corruption of good; yet it is parasitic on the good. In such a mythical conception evil is more positive than in monistic philosophies, and more dependent upon the good than in religious and philosophical dualisms. The myth of the Fall is thus in harmony with the mixture of profound pessimism and ultimate optimism which distinguishes prophetic religion from other forms of faith and other world-views. In the faith of prophetic religion existence is more certainly meaningful, its meaning is more definitely threatened by evil, and the triumph of good over evil is ultimately more certain than in alternative forms of religion.

It cannot be said that Christian orthodoxy has remained consistently true to these paradoxes of the myth of the Fall. They have always furnished a bulwark against more consistent and less profound analyses of the problem of evil; yet they have not been able wholly to prevent the waters of monism and dualism from seeping into Christian thought. With a correct intuition of the genius of its faith, Christian orthodoxy has always insisted that evil shall not be made good by attributing it to God; and that nature shall not be made evil by deriving sin from finiteness as such. Nevertheless fear of derogating from the omnipotence and majesty of God has frequently tempted Christian theologians into the error of declaring the Fall preordained in the counsels of God. John Calvin is, in a sense, typical of a tendency in Christian orthodoxy, in his provisional denial of God's responsibility for sin and his final acceptance of the idea, "Man falls, the providence of God so ordaining."[1] The omnipotence of God is the theologian's symbol of the basic and ultimate unity and coherence of the world and runs parallel to the monistic tendencies in philosophy. When unduly emphasized moral realism and vigour are sacrificed to the ideas of unity and consistency. Reason insists on a coherent world because it is its nature to relate all things to each other in one system of consistency and coherence. Morality, on the other hand, maintains its vigour only if the conflict between good and evil is recognized as real and significant. Luther, less philosophical than Calvin and more prophetic in temper, preserved the essential paradox more successfully. To him the devil was "God's devil." God used him to his own ends. "Devil," declares God in Luther's

---

[1] Calvin's *Institutes*, iii. 23:8.

words, "thou art a murderer and a criminal, but I will use thee for whatsoever I will. Thou shalt be the dung with which I will fertilize my lovely vineyard. I will and can use thee in my work on my vines. . . . Therefore thou mayst hack, cut, and destroy, but no further than I permit."[1] Luther significantly refused to develop the potential monism of such thought to a final and consistent conclusion.

Christian orthodoxy has had as much difficulty in escaping the Scylla of dualism as the Charybdis of monistic optimism. Sometimes, as in its theory of original sin, the finite world seems to be evil of itself, even though mortality is derived from sin and not sin from mortality. In the words of St Paul appear the significant mind-body distinction, "There dwelleth in me, that is in my flesh, no good thing." While it may be true, as many New Testament critics maintain, that the word flesh (sarx) had a symbolic rather than literal meaning for Paul, as the seat of evil, it is difficult to deny at least an echo of dualistic Greek mystery religions in this conception. At any rate, Christian life has frequently produced types of asceticism which can only be explained in terms of a dualistic influence upon, and corruption of, the original Hebraic mythical conception, the basis for which was probably laid by the profound insight in Hebrew thought of regarding soul and body as a unity and never separating them as later Greek thought tended to do.

The metaphysical connotations of the myth of the Fall are, however, less important for our purposes than the psychological and moral ones. It is in its interpretations of the facts of human nature, rather than in its oblique insights into the relation of order and chaos as such, that the myth of the Fall makes its profoundest contribution to moral and religious theory. The most basic and fruitful conception flowing from this ancient myth is the idea that evil lies at the juncture of nature and spirit. Evil is conceived as not simply the consequence of temporality or the fruit of nature's necessities. Sin can be understood neither in terms of the freedom of human reason alone, nor yet in terms of the circumscribed harmonies in which the human body is bound. Sin lies at the juncture of spirit and nature, in the sense that the peculiar and

---

[1] Quoted by Herman Obendiek, *Der Teufel bei Martin Luther*.

unique characteristics of human spirituality, in both its good and evil tendencies, can be understood only by analyzing the paradoxical relation of freedom and necessity, of finiteness and the yearning for the eternal in human life.

The fact that human finiteness stands under the perspective of the eternal and unconditioned and that the contingencies of the natural order are subjected to comparison with the ideal world of freedom explains why human beings cannot accept their limitations without a sense of guilt. The actions to which men are "driven" by necessities of the natural order are yet charged with guilt. While there are moral theories which deny this element of guilt, it is nevertheless a constant experience of human life and even when it is explicitly denied it is usually covertly affirmed. We never deal with our fellow-men as if they were only the irresponsible victims and instruments of the forces of nature and history.

Prophetic religion attributes moral evil to an evil will rather than to the limitations of natural man. That justification for such an emphasis lies in the fact that human reason is actually able to envisage moral possibilities, more inclusive loyalties, and more adequate harmonies of impulse and life in every instance of moral choice than those which are actually chosen. There is, therefore, an element of perversity, a conscious choice of the lesser good, involved in practically every moral action; and certainly there are some actions in which this conscious perversity is the dominant force of the action.

Yet in the Christian interpretation of moral evil guilt is attached not only to actions in which the individual is free to choose a higher possibility and fails to do so, but in which higher possibilities, which the individual is not free to choose, reveal the imperfection of the action which he is forced to take. Thus the simple moral guilt of conscious evil is transmuted into a sense of religious guilt which feels a general responsibility for that for which the individual agent cannot be immediately responsible. While the ascription of guilt to actions which are derived from the necessities of nature may lead to moral and religious morbidity, it is true, nevertheless, that moral complacency toward them is even more false to the human situation. Forces over which we have no control may drive our nation into war. Shall we accept all the moral alternatives which war makes inevitable as forced upon us by an ineluctable fate? A business man is forced to earn his livelihood within terms of an economic system in which perfect honesty would probably lead to self-destruction. According to the sensitivity of his spirit he will find some compromise between the immoral actions to which he is tempted by the necessities of the social system in which he operates and the ideal possibilities which his conscience projects. But there is no compromise at which he can rest complacently. Even though the highest moral possibility transcends the limits of his imperfect freedom, there is always an immediately higher possibility which he might take. A general sense of religious guilt is therefore a fruitful source of a sense of moral responsibility in immediate situations.

Thus, for instance, a question of equity between two individuals or social groups will elicit judgments from opposing sides at variance with each other, because each side sees the issues from a partial perspective; and the partiality of the perspective may be geographically determined. But the human mind is not completely bound by geographic limitations. In political controversies between America and Japan or between France and Russia, a developed intelligence has means of understanding and appreciating the viewpoint of the opposing side which transcend the limitations of time and place. If these should not suffice, there is always a limited possibility of changing the location from which the issue is viewed. A cloistered academic (to choose another example) can hardly be expected fully to appreciate the needs of the Negroes of Africa. The distance between himself and them is too great to allow such sympathies as manifest themselves in intimate communities and relations of contiguity to become effective. Yet when a cloistered academic like Albert Schweitzer, under a sense of responsibility for the needs of Africans and under a sense of guilt for the white man's sins against the coloured man, decides to expiate that guilt by casting his lot with the Africans on the edge of the primeval forest, he illustrates the freedom of spirit which transcends the limitations of nature. Because of this freedom the limitations cannot be accepted complacently. But neither must it be assumed, as it sometimes is in modern culture, that the progressive development of reason can completely overcome the partial insights and natural limits of finite men. Man, as the creature of both necessity and freedom, must, like Moses, always perish outside the promised land. He can see what he cannot reach.

The modern reaction to the religious sense of guilt has frequently tempted modern culture to deny the idea of moral responsibility completely. This was natural enough because modern culture is under the influence of the scientific method; and no scientific description of a moral act can ever disclose the area of freedom in which alternative choices are weighed. A scientific description of an act is both external and retrospective. For it every act is deterministically related to previous acts and conditions in an endless chain of natural causes and effects. Thus the delinquency of an adolescent boy can be scientifically related to an unsatisfactory environment or to the premature death of the father, or to adenoids, or to a deficiency of iodine in his diet. The social sciences can in fact compile statistics proving a conclusive relationship between premature parental deaths and juvenile delinquency. But none of these statistics will help in determining, before rather than after, the event, whether the untimely death of a father will cause an adolescent boy to become a problem or will nerve him to achieve a premature maturity. To an external observer no conscious choice of evil is ever discernible. There is always a previous condition or the force of an antecedent impulse which seems to offer a complete explanation of the inevitability of the act.

The full dimension of depth in which all human actions transpire is disclosed only in introspection. An intense type of introspection is always a religious experience because in it the possibilities of good and evil, between which human choices are made, are fully disclosed. The heights and depths of the world of spirit are measured. In its most developed form it discloses possibilities of both good and evil which in one moment seem to be alternative forces within the self and in the next are recognized as forces which transcend the self. Therefore no limits can be set where the self ends and either nature or the divine begins, a fact accurately stated in the two contrasting words of St Paul, "I, yet not I, but Christ who liveth in me," and, "It is no more I that do it, but sin that dwelleth in me." The full dimension of the self includes, on the one hand, possibilities not present in the world of actuality at all, and on the other hand a "dark and cavernous background in which the perspectives of the self's living past merge insensibly with the vast shapes of physical nature."[1]

It is interesting that common-sense moral judgments never adopt the scientific account of a moral act consistently. They always introduce the factor of freedom and responsibility, which the act of the other does not disclose to the observer, but which the latter adds from his own introspective experience. Even as rigorous a determinist as Karl Marx, who at times described the social behaviour of the bourgeoisie in terms which suggested a problem in social physics, could subject it at other times to a withering scorn which only the presupposition of moral responsibility could justify. It is interesting to note in this connection that while Marxism is anxious to reduce the processes of human consciousness to terms which would relate them to the "laws of motion" in the physical world[2] the strategy of communist parties always includes the charge of moral dishonesty against its foes.

While common sense maintains the idea of moral responsibility for human actions and attaches moral guilt to anti-social actions, a high religion goes beyond common sense in that it excludes no action, not even the best, for the feeling of guilt. This result is due to the fact that religion sees all reality, including human personality, in such a dimension of depth, that some transcendent possibility always stands above every actuality, as a vantage-point from which actual achievements are found wanting. Thus the ideal of perfect love gives a perspective upon every human action which prompts the confession, "Are we not all unprofitable servants?"

While rational and non-mythical religions tend to define the ideal in terms of passionless form and the world of actuality as unqualifiedly evil, it is the virtue of mythical religions that they discover symbols of the transcendent in the actual without either separating the one from, or identifying it with, the other. This is perhaps the most essential genius of myth, that it points to the timeless in time, to the ideal in the actual, but does not lift the temporal to the category of the eternal (as pantheism does), nor

---

[1] W. E. Hocking, *The Self, Its Body and Its Freedom*, p. 110.
[2] Engels wrote: "That the material conditions of life of the men in whose heads the thinking process takes place ultimately determine the course of the process necessarily remains unknown to them, otherwise there would be an end of the whole ideology."

deny the significant glimpses of the eternal and the ideal in the temporal (as dualism does). When the mythical method is applied to the description of human character, its paradoxes disclose precisely the same relationships in human personality which myth reveals, and more consistent philosophies obscure, in the nature of the universe. The quintessence of a human personality is never in time or historic actuality. Yet it is the unifying principle in the whole welter of impulses which operate in the natural level. That is why the secret of a personality is never fully disclosed and also why the artist is more successful in discovering clues to it than the scientist. If the artist is to symbolize what he has discovered he is forced to avail himself of mythical technique, the portrait, for instance. The distinctions between a portrait and a photograph are typical of the differences between myth and science. In the latter immediate actualities are faithfully and accurately recorded; but the mood of the moment which the photograph catches may obscure or falsify the quintessential spirit of a personality. The portrait artist, on the other hand, will falsify, unduly accentuate, and select physiognamic details in order to present his vision of the transcendent unity and spirit of the personality. The vagueness of the boundary line between the art of portraiture and that of caricature suggests how difficult it is to distinguish between deception in the interest of a higher truth and deception which falsifies the ultimate truth.

It is by its mythical approach to the problems of the human spirit that prophetic religion is able to preserve a dynamic ethic and not fall into the pitfall of a romantic glorification of impulse; and can subject dynamic and impulsive life to transcendent criteria without creating a passionless other-worldliness. The difference between the Buddhistic and Christian conception of love is the difference between a rational and a mythical approach. In Buddhism love is affirmed as a principle of unity and harmony, but disavowed as a dynamic impulse. Buddhism is, therefore, unable to escape an enervating ambiguity in its statement of the love ideal.

According to the prophetic conception, moral evil lies at the juncture of nature and spirit. The reality of moral guilt is asserted because the forces and impulses of nature never move by absolute necessity, but under and in the freedom of the spirit. But the myth of the Fall involves more than this assertion of moral responsibility. It involves a definition of, or at least clues to, the character of moral evil in man. Sin is rebellion against God. If finiteness cannot be without guilt because it is mixed with freedom and stands under ideal possibilities, it cannot be without sin (in the more exact sense of the term) because man makes pretensions of being absolute in his finiteness. He tries to translate his finite existence into a more permanent and absolute form of existence. Ideally men seek to subject their arbitrary and contingent existence under the dominion of absolute reality. But practically they always mix the finite with the eternal and claim for themselves, their nation, their culture, or their class the centre of existence. This is the root of all imperialism in man and explains why the restricted predatory impulses of the animal world are transmuted into the boundless imperial ambitions of human life. Thus the moral urge to establish order in life is mixed with the ambition to make oneself the centre of that order; and devotion to every transcendent value is corrupted by the effort to insert the interests of the self into that value. The organizing centre of life and history must transcend life and history, since everything which appears in time and history is too partial and incomplete to be its centre. But man is destined, both by the imperfection of his knowledge and by his desire to overcome his finiteness to make absolute claims for his partial and finite values. He tries, in short, to make himself God.

This explanation of the matter not only emphasizes the spiritual, rather than natural, character of human evil, but also involves the doctrine of its inevitability. The most ideal aspirations of the human spirit always contain an alloy of idealizing pretensions. The higher the aspirations rise the more do sinful pretensions accompany them. Modern nations are probably more desirous of universal peace than primitive nations. The latter asserted their collective will against other groups without interest in an ultimate harmony of nations. But modern nations are both more desirous of peace and more ambitious to impose their peace upon the world. Thus Stoic universalism and Roman imperialism grew together; and in our own era the universalistic dreams of the French Revolution resulted immediately in Napoleonic imperialism and ultimately in the brutal thrust of the white man's empire into the more vegetative and less "spiritual" portions of the globe.

In the myth of the Fall God is pictured as a jealous God who seeks to withhold the fruit of the tree of knowledge from man. The serpent seeks to discredit the motives of God as pure jealousy: "For God doth know that in the day ye eat thereof, then your eyes shall be opened; and ye shall be as gods, knowing good and evil." The Promethean myth of the Homeric saga has a similar motif, though in it the jealous God seeks to throttle, not the knowledge of good and evil, but the achievements of applied science—*i.e.*, man's ability to conquer the forces of nature.

The inability of modern culture to see no more in the notion of a jealous God than the expression of a primitive fear of the higher powers, is another indication of its superficiality. The very crux of the spiritual problem of man is broadly suggested in this myth. God is necessarily jealous because the root of man's sin lies in his pretension of being God. This pretension would be impossible if man were not created in the "image of God"—*i.e.*, if he did not have capacities for self-transcendence which permitted him to see his finite existence under the perspective of its eternal essence. But it would also be impossible if man's finiteness did not betray him into a corruption of the highest values. This corruption is not due simply to the fact that finite men fail to see far enough, or to envisage reality widely enough, to comprehend the actual centre of life. It is also due to the fact that men are tempted to protest against their finiteness by seeking to make themselves infinite. Thus evil in its most developed form is always a good which imagines itself, or pretends to be, better than it is. The devil is always an angel who pretends to be God. Therefore, while egoism is the driving force of sin, dishonesty is its final expression. The heart of this matter is well expressed in the Slavonic Enoch where the origin of evil is described as follows:

> And one from out of the order of angels, having turned away from the order that was under him, conceived an impossible thought, to place his throne higher than the clouds above the earth, that he might become equal with my (*i.e.* God's) rank. And I threw him out of the height with his angels.[1]

There is always a possibility, not to be overlooked, that the idea of a jealous God who seeks to prevent men from gaining the

---

[1] Quoted by N. P. Williams, *The Ideas of the Fall and of Original Sin*, p. 161.

knowledge of good and evil expresses a darkly unconscious human fear of the very adventure of human existence. A God, jealous to preserve man in his primeval state of innocency, is a conception which may express the idea that, since every human advance offers new possibilities of catastrophe and every virtue has the possibilities of a vicious aberration in it, it were better for man if he could return to his original state, or, as the psychoanalysts phrase it, if he could return to the womb. Such fears are expressed in a multitude of ancient myths, and they have at least this justification that the adventure of life is much more perilous than is assumed by those who imagine that human rationality is a simple guarantee of progressive moral achievement.

That the basic motive of the myth of the Fall, expressed in the idea of the jealous God and the human rebellion against the divine, is not the fruit of primitive fantasy but a revelation of a tragic reality of life, is attested by every page of human history. Every conceivable social peace which men have attained and toward which they still strive, is always something of a Pax Romana. Necessary social order can actually be established; but it is never pure peace, pure justice, and pure order. The roots of anarchy are bound to be in it because it is always a peace which pretends to be more than it is. It is a peace imposed by some human instrument of order; and in that human instrument is an imperial ambition, hiding its will to power under the veil of its will to peace. The peace of the world, the more inclusive harmonies of human existence, are maintained by Roman arms, or by the League of Nations (which means the dominant powers), or by the commercial and industrial oligarchy which ruled the nations in the past decades, or by a communist oligarchy of the future (which may achieve a higher and juster peace, but which will also make more absolute and therefore more demonic pretensions). The more orderly and more highly integrated civilizations conquer the more anarchic social units, as Great Britain dominates India and Japan will continue to encroach upon China. All this is done in the interest of order and harmony and is therefore supposedly virtuous. But it is not as virtuous as it pretends to be; and also less virtuous than it might be if it made fewer pretensions. Yet the pretensions spring inevitably out of the human situation.

It is possible for individuals to be saved from this sinful pretension, not by achieving an absolute perspective upon life, but by their recognition of their inability to do so. Individuals may be saved by repentance, which is the gateway to grace. The recognition of creatureliness and finiteness, in other words, may become the basis of man's reconciliation to God through his resignation to his finite condition. But the collective life of mankind promises no such hope of salvation, for the very reason that it offers men the very symbols of pseudo-universality which tempt them to glorify and worship themselves as God.

The pessimism of this analysis is akin to that of the orthodox conception of "original sin." Unfortunately, Christian orthodoxy has usually bedevilled this doctrine by trying to construct a history of sin out of the concept of its inevitability. The vice of all mythical religion is that its interpreters try to reduce its supra-history to actual history. Thus the myth of creation is constructed into an actual history of origins when it is really a description of the quality of existence. The myth of the Fall is made into an account of the origin of evil, when it is really a description of its nature. The orthodox doctrine of "original sin" is an effort to extend the history of sin from its origin through successive generations of mankind. It therefore becomes a doctrine of an "inherited corruption," the precise nature of which could significantly never be found by theologians, but which they most frequently identified with the sexual lust, attendant upon the process of generation. If original sin is an inherited corruption, its inheritance destroys the freedom and therefore the responsibility which is basic to the conception of sin. The orthodox doctrine is therefore self-destructive. Augustine faced this problem, but could not solve it within terms of his presuppositions. Original sin is not an inherited corruption, but it is an inevitable fact of human existence, the inevitability of which is given by the nature of man's spirituality. It is true in every moment of existence, but it has no history.

The orthodox doctrine of a "total depravity," resulting from a complete corruption of the "image of God" in man, is equally destructive of the very insight which it seeks to perfect. This type of pessimism is developed most consistently in Augustinian-Lutheran theology. Thus the Lutheran "Formulary of Concord" condemns the "synergists" because "they teach that our nature has been greatly weakened and corrupted because of the fall of the human race, but nevertheless has not lost all its goodness. . . . For they say that from natural birth man still has remaining somewhat of good, however little, minute, scanty, and attenuated it may be."[1] Calvin, with greater insight, refused to admit the total corruption of reason. The human capacity for self-transcendence, the ability to see beyond an immediate world to more and more inclusive loyalties and values, is the basis of all that is good and all that is evil in human life. If it were altogether evil and corrupt, it could not become the basis of the kind of evil for which men feel themselves responsible. It is human freedom, in other words, created by the transcendence of reason over impulse, which makes sin possible. Therefore, if man is totally corrupt he is not sinful at all. At any rate, sin has been stripped of the connotation of guilt, or guilt has been divested of the implication of moral responsibility.

On this important problem Augustinian Christianity and modern culture have both failed to grasp the paradoxical relation of spirit and nature, of reason and impulse, in human wrong-doing. The former fails to make a significant distinction between reason and impulse and the latter erroneously sees in reason the unqualified basis of virtue and in impulse the root of all evil. The former theory obscures the fact that a significant portion of human wrong-doing is due to human finiteness. This finiteness includes both the imperfect vision of human reason and the blindness of human impulse. There are not always imperial or demonic pretensions in the evil which flows from such finiteness. The anarchy which results from such evil is more like the anarchies which exist in the natural world, where the individual life does not try to make itself the centre of existence, but merely makes itself the centre of its own existence. Since no discrete and atomic individual life exists anywhere in nature or human history, such self-centred existence always disturbs the harmony and inter-relatedness of existence. It is, nevertheless, a different order and level of evil from the spiritual evil which is the consequence of trying to make the self the centre of existence. It is this latter type

---

[1] Quoted by N. P. Williams, *op. cit.*, p. 428.

of evil which is sin in the strictest sense of the word. It is here that the rebellion against God is committed which high religion has always regarded as the essence of sin. The distinction between sin and weakness is in the degree of this pretension and, not incidentally, as some modern theologians would have it, in the degree of conscious rejection of the good.[1]

Because Augustinian Christianity does not make the distinction between finiteness as such and the sin which flows from the divine pretensions of finite creatures, it failed to strengthen the rational sources of virtue and led to the protest of the Age of Reason and modern culture. While this protest resulted in an equally dangerous identification of reason and virtue, it did have the merit of encouraging all the various forms of modern social education which aim at a greater harmony of life with life. One of the vices of a really profound religion is that its insights into the ultimate problems of the human spirit frequently betray it into indifference toward the immediate problems of justice and equity in human relations. Against this tendency it must be insisted that the degree of imagination and insight with which disciplined minds are able to enter into the problems of their fellow-men and to enlarge the field of interests in which human actions take place, may materially improve human happiness and social harmony. A religious ethic which holds such achievements in contempt discredits itself particularly in a generation in which the problems of man's aggregate existence have become so difficult and the evils of social misunderstandings so great, that their slightest alleviation must be regarded as a boon to mankind.

In modern culture, on the other hand, the unqualified identification of reason and virtue has led to untold evils and confusions. Against the illusions of modern culture it must be maintained that the natural impulses of life are not so anarchic and reason is not so unqualifiedly synthetizing as has been assumed. While natural impulse, without the discipline of reason, may lead to anarchy in the self and in society, it must also be recognized that there are natural social impulses which relate the self to other life in terms of an unconscious and natural harmony. This virtue of nature may be destroyed by rationality. "The

---

[1] Cf., *inter alia*, Tennant, *The Concept of Sin*, p. 245 ff.

native hue of resolution" which is "sicklied o'er by a pale cast of thought" may be some prompting of natural impulse, as, for instance, a mother's concern for her child or the emotion of pity for the distress of another. Thus simple people frequently achieve or possess virtues of tenderness which elude the wise, who know all about Aristotle's (or Irving Babbitt's) "law of measure." "Primitive religion," declares Henri Bergson "is a precaution against the danger man runs, as soon as he thinks at all, of thinking of himself alone. It is therefore, a defensive reaction of nature against intelligence."[1]

Intelligence may enervate moral action not only by strengthening egoistic impulses against the force of instinctive sociality, but by setting any conceivable value in balance against every conceivable value until action becomes impossible, or finally by transmuting the narrow harmonies of nature into wider harmonies, which are, however, not wide or broad enough to do justice to the whole social situation. The same intelligence which operates to introduce harmony into the anarchy of impulse also creates anarchies upon higher levels. Only a nation which has achieved internal harmony and integration and has the imaginative capacity to look beyond its borders can be imperialistic. Only adults and mature nations are prompted in their dealings with others by stubborn vindictiveness. Vengeance requires memory, and memory is an achievement of intelligence. Animals, children, and primitive nations have short memories. Hence their resentments are quickly dissipated. Only highly cultured nations like Germany and France allow the accumulated resentments of the centuries to determine their present policies.

It is this aspect of man's spiritual problem which modern culture does not understand. This failure of understanding imparts an air of sentimentality and illusion to all modern moral and social theories, whether liberal or radical. So pervasive is the optimism and unilateral simplicity of modern morality that even an Anglo-Catholic theologian, under its influence, can arrive at the foolish conclusion that the Christian conception of love is practically identical with the "herd complex"; so that St. Paul's confession about "the sin that dwelleth in me" is translated to mean "the innate weakness of my herd instinct." In conformity

[1] Henri Bergson, *The Two Sources of Religion and Morality*, p. 113.

with modern opinion sin is regarded as "nothing but a defect, a gap, a blank, a minus quantity."[1] It is assumed in such an analysis that the herd complex gradually develops until it includes the whole of society and becomes identical with "moral sentiment" in general. Such a superficial analysis does not do justice to the fact that the most stubborn evil in human life appears precisely at the point where the forces which make for community have been extended far enough to create large social aggregates which are not large enough to include the total human community and are yet powerful enough to dominate and destroy life beyond themselves.

When, as in Freudian psychology, modern culture becomes aware of the more tragic aspects of human society and rejects the simple and optimistic analyses of yesterday, failure to understand the dialectical relationship of good and evil, betrays it into a new kind of dualism, in which the human psyche is divided not between mind and impulse, but between two types of impulse, diametrically opposed to each other, Freud writes: "The process (of culture) proves to be in the service of Eros, which aims at binding together single human individuals, then families, then tribes, races, nations, into one great unity, that of humanity. Why this has to be done we do not know. It is simply the work of Eros. These masses of men must be bound to one another libidinally; necessity alone, the advantages of common work, would not hold them together. The natural instinct of aggressiveness in man, the hostility of each one against all and of all against each one, opposes this programme of civilization. This instinct is the derivative and the main representative of the death instinct we have found alongside of Eros, sharing his rule over the earth. And now, it seems to me, the meaning of the evolution of culture is no longer a riddle to us. It must present to us the struggle between Eros and Death, between the instincts of life and the instincts of destruction, as it works itself out in the human species. This struggle is what all life consists of essentially and so the evolution of civilization may be described as the struggle of the human species for existence. And it is this battle of Titans that our nurses and governesses try to compose with their lullaby song of Heaven."[2]

These supposedly profound words, which pretentiously offer a

---

[1] N. P. Williams, *op. cit.*, pp. 480-482.
[2] Sigmund Freud, *Civilization and its Discontents*, pp. 102-103.

clue to the meaning of "the evolution of culture" throw little light on the actual human situation. Their only merit is to be found in their challenge to the "lullaby songs" of our "nurses and governesses." The idea that a separate and distinct death impulse operates mysteriously in conflict with the life impulse has the virtue of calling attention to the dynamic character of evil in the world. But every social situation proves that an impulse of sheer destruction exists only among psycho-pathics. In normal life the death impulse is in the service of the life impulse or flows from it inadvertently. Neither animals nor men kill out of sheer love of destruction. They kill to maintain their own life. They destroy the foe only when he challenges the community which Eros has established. Evil, in other words, is much more inextricably bound up with good than is comprehended in this psychology or in any of the modern substitutes for the analysis of prophetic Christianity. Even if the death impulse were as pure as Freud assumes it to be, it could be gratified successfully only by a group bound together in a powerful libidinal cohesion, to use his phrase.

The Christian analysis of life leads to conclusions which will seem morbidly pessimistic to moderns, still steeped as they are in their evolutionary optimism. The conclusion most abhorrent to the modern mood is that the possibilities of evil grow with the possibilities of good, and that human history is therefore not so much a chronicle of the progressive victory of the good over evil, of cosmos over chaos, as the story of an ever-increasing cosmos, creating ever-increasing possibilities of chaos. The idea hinted at in the words of St Paul, "For I had not known lust, except the law had said thou shalt not covet,"[1] the idea, namely, that when the moral ideal challenges the forces of sin, the challenge results not only in submission, but to a more conscious and deliberate opposition, is proved by the tragic facts of human history, however unpalatable it may be to generations which have tried to explain human history in simpler terms.

Naturally, it is not easy to elaborate an adequate ethic for the immediate social problems of human existence in terms of the tension created by Christian love perfectionism on the one hand, and this kind of realism on the other. In the more mystical and dualistic religions this tension of high religion breaks and mun-

[1] Romans vii. 7.

dane existence sinks into meaninglessness. Even in Christianity, in spite of its prophetic inheritance, this has frequently been the consequence of the tension. Our modern culture, which views human life only in terms of a single dimension was, from this perspective, a justified protest against a religion which betrayed men into indifference toward the immediate problems of their historical and social existence. But since the vertical dimension in human life, revealing the ultimate possibilities of good and the depths of evil in it, is a reality which naïve philosophies may obscure but cannot destroy, it will be necessary for our generation to return to the faith of prophetic Christianity to solve its problems. At the same time it will be necessary for prophetic Christianity, with a stronger emphasis upon its prophetic and a lesser emphasis upon its rationalistic inheritance, to develop a more adequate social ethic within terms of its understanding of the total human situation. The approach of the historic Christian Church to the moral issues of life has been less helpful than it might have been, partly because a literal interpretation of its mythical basis destroyed the genius of prophetic religion, and partly because Christianity, in the effort to rationalize its myths, ran upon the rocks either of the Scylla of a too optimistic pantheism or the Charybdis of a too pessimistic and other-worldly dualism.

4

THE RELEVANCE OF AN IMPOSSIBLE ETHICAL IDEAL

Prophetic Christianity faces the difficulty that its penetration into the total and ultimate human situation complicates the problem of dealing with the immediate moral and social situations which all men must face. The common currency of the moral life is constituted of the "nicely calculated less and more" of the relatively good and the relatively evil. Human happiness in ordinary intercourse is determined by the difference between a little more and a little less justice, a little more and little less freedom, between varying degrees of imaginative insight with which the self enters the life and understands the interests of the neighbour. Prophetic Christianity, on the other hand, demands the impossible; and by that very demand emphasizes the impotence and corruption of human nature, wresting from man the cry of distress and contrition, "The good that I would, do I do not: but the evil that I would not, that I do. . . . Woe is me . . . who will deliver me from the body of this death." Measuring the distance between mountain peaks and valleys and arriving at the conclusion that every high mountain has a "timber line" above which life cannot maintain itself, it is always tempted to indifference toward the task of building roads up the mountain-side, and of coercing its wilderness into a sufficient order to sustain human life. The latter task must consequently be assumed by those who are partly blind to the total dimension of life and, being untouched by its majesties and tragedies, can give themselves to the immediate tasks before them.

Thus prophetic religion tends to disintegrate into two contrasting types of religion. The one inclines to deny the relevance of the ideal of love, to the ordinary problems of existence, certain that the tragedy of human life must be resolved by something more than moral achievement. The other tries to prove the relevance of the religious ideal to the problems of everyday existence by reducing it to conformity with the prudential rules of conduct which the common sense of many generations and the experience of the ages have elaborated. Broadly speaking, the conflict between orthodox Christianity and modern secularism. In so far as liberal Christianity is a compound of prophetic religion and secularism it is drawn into the debate in a somewhat equivocal position but, on the whole, on the side of the secularists and naturalists.

Against orthodox Christianity, the prophetic tradition in Christianity must insist on the relevance of the ideal of love to the moral experience of mankind of every conceivable level. It is not an ideal magically superimposed upon life by a revelation which has no relation to total human experience. The whole conception of life revealed in the Cross of Christian faith is not a pure negation of , or irrelevance toward, the moral ideals of "natural man." While the final heights of the love ideal condemn as well as fulfil the moral canons of common sense, the ideal is involved in every moral aspiration and achievement. It is the genius and the task of prophetic religion to insist on the organic relation between historic human existence and that which is both the ground and the fulfilment of this existence, the transcendent.

Moral life is possible at all only in a meaningful existence. Obligation can be felt only to some system of coherence and some ordering will. Thus moral obligation is always an obligation to promote harmony and to overcome chaos. But every conceivable order in the historical world contains an element of anarchy. Its world rests upon contingency and caprice. The obligation to support and enhance it can therefore only arise and maintain itself upon the basis of a faith that it is the partial fruit of a deeper unity and the promise of a more perfect harmony than is revealed in any immediate situation. If a lesser faith than this prompts moral action, it results in precisely those types of moral fanaticism which impart unqualified worth to qualified values and thereby destroy even their qualified worth. The prophetic faith in a God who is both the ground and the ultimate fulfilment of existence, who is both the creator and the judge of the world, is thus involved in every moral situation. Without it the world is seen either as being meaningless or as revealing unqualifiedly good and simple meanings. In either case the nerve of moral action is ultimately destroyed. The dominant attitudes of prophetic faith are gratitude and contrition; gratitude for Creation and contrition before Judgment; or, in other words, confidence that life is good in spite of its evil and that it is evil in spite of its good. In such a faith both sentimentality and despair are avoided. The meaningfulness of life does not tempt to premature complacency, and the chaos which always threatens the world of meaning does not destroy the tension of faith and hope in which all moral action is grounded.

The prophetic faith, that the meaningfulness of life and existence implies a source and end beyond itself, produces a morality which implies that every moral value and standard is grounded in and points toward an ultimate perfection of unity and harmony, not realizable in any historic situation. An analysis of the social history of mankind validates this interpretation.

In spite of the relativity of morals every conceivable moral code and every philosophy of morals enjoins concern for the life and welfare of the other and seeks to restrain the unqualified assertion of the interests of the self against the other. There is thus a fairly universal agreement in all moral systems that it is wrong to take the life or the property of the neighbour, though it must be admitted that the specific applications of these general principles vary greatly according to time and place. This minimal standard of moral conduct is grounded in the law of love and points toward it as ultimate fulfilment. The obligation to affirm and protect the life of others can arise at all only if it is assumed that life is related to life in some unity and harmony of existence. In any given instance motives of the most calculating prudence rather than a high sense of obligation may enforce the standard. Men may defend the life of the neighbour merely to preserve those processes of mutuality by which their own life is protected. But that only means that they have discovered the inter-relatedness of life through concern for themselves rather than by an analysis of the total situation. This purely prudential approach will not prompt the most consistent social conduct, but it will nevertheless implicitly affirm what it ostensibly denies—that the law of life is love.

Perhaps the clearest proof that the law of love is involved as a basis of even the most minimal social standards, is found in the fact that every elaboration of minimal standards into higher standards makes the implicit relation more explicit. Prohibitions of murder and theft are negative. They seek to prevent one life from destroying or taking advantage of another. No society is content with these merely negative prohibitions. Its legal codes do not go much beyond negatives because only minimal standards can be legally enforced. But the moral codes and ideals of every advanced society demand more than mere prohibition of theft and murder. Higher conceptions of justice are developed. It is recognized that the right to live implies the right to secure the goods which sustain life. This right immediately involves more than mere prohibition of theft. Some obligation is felt, however dimly, to organize the common life so that the neighbour will have fair opportunities to maintain his life. The various schemes of justice and equity which grow out of this obligation, consciously or unconsciously imply an ideal of equality beyond themselves. Equality is always the regulative principle of justice; and in the ideal of equality there is an echo of the law of love, "Thou shalt love thy neighbour AS THYSELF." If the question is raised to what degree the neighbour has a right to support his life through the privileges and opportunities of the common life, no satisfactory, rational answer can be given to it, short of one implying equalitarian principles: He has just as much right as you yourself.

This does not mean that any society will ever achieve perfect equality. Equality, being a rational, political version of the law of love, shares with it the quality of transcendence. It ought to be, but it never will be fully realized. Social prudence will qualify it. The most equalitarian society will probably not be able to dispense with special rewards as inducements to diligence. Some differentials in privilege will be necessary to make the performance of certain social functions possible. While a rigorous equalitarian society can prevent such privileges from being perpetuated from one generation to another without regard to social function, it cannot eliminate privileges completely. Nor is there any political technique which would be a perfect guarantee against abuses of socially sanctioned privileges. Significant social functions are endowed by their very nature with a certain degree of social power. Those who possess power, however socially restrained, always have the opportunity of deciding that the function which they perform is entitled to more privilege than any ideal scheme of justice would allow. The ideal of equality is thus qualified in any possible society by the necessities of social cohesion and corrupted by the sinfulness of men. It remains, nevertheless, a principle of criticism under which every scheme of justice stands and a symbol of the principle of love involved in all moral judgments.

But the principle of equality does not exhaust the possibilities of the moral ideal involved in even the most minimal standards of justice. Imaginative justice leads beyond equality to a consideration of the special needs of the life of the other. A sensitive parent will not make capricious distinctions in the care given to different children. But the kind of imagination which governs the most ideal family relationships soon transcends this principle of equality and justifies special care for a handicapped child and, possibly, special advantages for a particularly gifted one. The "right" to have others consider one's unique needs and potentialities is recognized legally only in the most minimal terms and is morally recognized only in very highly developed communities. Yet the modern public school, which began with the purpose of providing equal educational opportunities for all children, has extended its services so that both handicapped and highly gifted children receive special privileges from it. Every one of these achievements in the realm of justice is logically related, on the one hand, to the most minimal standards of justice, and on the other to the ideal of perfect love—*i.e.*, to the obligation of affirming the life and interests of the neighbour as much as those of the self. The basic rights to life and property in the early community, the legal minima of rights and obligations of more advanced communities, the moral rights and obligations recognized in these communities beyond those which are legally enforced, the further refinement of standards in the family beyond those recognized in the general community—all these stand in an ascending scale of moral possibilities in which each succeeding step is a closer approximation of the law of love.

The history of corrective justice reveals the same ascending scale of possibilities as that of distributive justice. Society begins by regulating vengeance and soon advances to the stage of substituting public justice for private vengeance. Public justice recognizes the right of an accused person to a more disinterested judgment than that of the injured accuser. Thus the element of vengeance is reduced, but not eliminated, in modern standards of punitive justice. The same logic which forced its reduction presses on toward its elimination. The criminal is recognized to have rights as a human being, even when he has violated his obligations to society. Therefore modern criminology, using psychiatric techniques, seeks to discover the cause of anti-social conduct in order that it may be corrected. The reformatory purpose attempts to displace the purely punitive intent. This development follows a logic which must culminate in the command, "Love your enemies." The more imaginative ideals of the best criminologists are, of course, in the realm of unrealized hopes. They will never be fully realized. An element of vindictive passion will probably corrupt the corrective justice of even the best society. The collective behaviour is not imaginative enough to assure more than minimal approximations of the ideal. Genuine forgiveness of the enemy requires a contrite recognition of the sinfulness of the self and of the mutual responsibility for the sin of the accused. Such spiritual penetration is beyond the capacities of collective man. It is the achievement of only rare individuals. Yet the right to such understanding is involved in the most basic of human rights and follows logically if the basic right to life is rationally elaborated. Thus all standards of corrective justice are organically related to primitive vengeance on the one hand, and the ideal of forgiving love on the other. No absolute limit can be placed upon the degree to which human society may yet approximate the ideal. But it is certain that every achievement will remain in the realm of approximation. The ideal in its perfect form lies beyond the capacities of human nature.

Moral and social ideals are always a part of a series of infinite possibilities not only in terms of their purity, but in terms of their breadth of application. The most tender and imaginative human attitudes are achieved only where consanguinity and contiguity support the unity of life with life, and nature aids spirit in creating harmony. Both law and morality recognize rights and obligations within the family which are not recognized in the community, and within the community which are not accepted beyond the community. Parents are held legally responsible for the neglect of their children but not for the neglect of other people's children. Modern nations assume qualified responsibilities for the support of their unemployed, but not for the unemployed of other nations. Such a sense of responsibility may be too weak to function adequately without the support of political motives, as, for instance, the fear that hungry men may disturb the social peace. But weak as it is, it is yet strong enough to suggest responsibilities beyond itself. No modern people is completely indifferent toward the responsibility for all human life. In terms of such breadth the obligation is too weak to become the basis for action, except on rare occasions. The need of men in other nations must be vividly portrayed and dramatized by some great catastrophe before generosity across national boundaries expresses itself. But it can express itself, even in those rare moments, only because all human life is informed with an inchoate sense of responsibility toward the ultimate law of life—the law of love. The community of mankind has no organs of social cohesion and no instruments for enforcing social standards (and it may never have more than embryonic ones); yet that community exists in a vague sense of responsibility toward all men which underlies all moral responsibilities in limited communities.

As has been observed in analyzing the ethic of Jesus, the universalism of prophetic ethics goes beyond the demands of rational universalism. In rational universalism obligation is felt to all life because human life is conceived as the basic value of ethics. Since so much of human life represents only potential value, rational universalism tends to qualify its position. Thus in Aristotelian ethics the slave does not have the same rights as the freeman because his life is regarded as of potentially less value. Even in Stoicism, which begins by asserting the common divinity of all men by reason of their common rationality, the obvious differences in the intelligence of man prompts Stoic doctrine to a certain aristocratic condescension toward the "fools." In prophetic religion the obligation is toward the loving will of God; in other words, toward a more transcendent source of unity than any discoverable in the natural world, where men are always divided by various forces of nature and history. Christian universalism, therefore, represents a more impossible possibility than the universalism of Stoicism. Yet it is able to prompt higher actualities of love, being less dependent upon obvious symbols of human unity and brotherhood. In prophetic ethics the transcendent unity of life is an article of faith. Moral obligation is to this divine unity; and therefore it is more able to defy the anarchies of the world. But this difference between prophetic and rational universalism must not obscure a genuine affinity. In both cases the moral experience on any level of life points toward an unrealizable breadth of obligation of life to life.

If further proof were needed of the relevance of the love commandment to the problems of ordinary morality it could be found by a negative argument: Natural human egoism, which is sin only from the perspective of the law of love, actually results in social consequences which prove this religious perspective to be right. This point must be raised not against Christian orthodoxy, which has never denied this negative relevance of the law of love to all human situations, but against a naturalism which regards the law of love as an expression of a morbid perfectionism, and declares "we will not aim so high or fall so low." According to the thesis of modern naturalism, only excessive egoism can be called wrong. The natural self-regarding impulses of human nature are accepted as the data of ethics; and the effort is made to construct them into forces of social harmony and cohesion. Prophetic Christianity, unlike modern liberalism, knows that the force of egoism cannot be broken by moral suasion and that on certain levels qualified harmonies must be achieved by building conflicting egoisms into a balance of power. But, unlike modern naturalism, it is unable to adopt a complacent attitude toward the force of egoism. It knows that it is sin, however natural and inevitable it may be, and its sinfulness is proved by the social consequences. It is natural enough to love one's own family more than other families and no amount of education will ever eliminate the inverse ratio between the potency of love and the breadth and extension in which it is applied. But the inevitability of narrow loyalties and circumscribed sympathy does not destroy the moral and social peril which they create. A narrow family loyalty is a more potent source of injustice than pure individual egoism, which, incidentally, probably never exists. The special loyalty which men give their limited community is natural enough; but it is also the root of international anarchy. Moral idealism in terms of the presuppositions of a particular class is also natural and inevitable; but it is the basis of tyranny and hypocrisy. Nothing is more natural and, in a sense, virtuous, than the desire of parents to protect the future of their children by bequeathing the fruits of their own toil and fortune to them. Yet this desire results in laws of testation by which social privilege is divorced from social function. The social injustice and conflicts of human history spring neither from a pure egoism nor from the type of egoism which could be neatly measured as excessive or extravagant by some rule of reason. They spring from those virtuous attitudes of natural man in which natural sympathy is inevitably compounded with natural egoism. Not only excessive jealousy, but the ordinary jealousy, from which no soul is free, destroys the harmony of life with life. Not only excessive vengeance, but the subtle vindictiveness which insinuates itself into the life of even the most imaginative souls destroys justice. Wars are the consequence of the moral attitudes not only of unrighteous but of righteous nations (righteous in the sense that they defend their interests no more than is permitted by all the moral codes of history). The judgment that "whosoever seeketh to gain his life will lose it" remains true and relevant to every moral situation even if it is apparent that no human being exists who does not in some sense lose his life by seeking to gain it.

A naturalistic ethics, incapable of comprehending the true dialectic of the spiritual life, either regards the love commandment as possible of fulfilment and thus slips into utopianism, or it is forced to relegate it to the category of an either harmless or harmful irrelevance. A certain type of Christian liberalism interprets the absolutism of the ethics of the sermon on the mount as Oriental hyperbole, as a harmless extravagance, possessing a certain value in terms of pedagogical emphasis. A purely secular naturalism, on the other hand, considers the absolutism as a harmful extravagance. Thus Sigmund Freud writes: "The cultural super-ego . . . does not trouble enough about the mental constitution of human beings; it enjoins a command and never asks whether it is possible for them to obey it. It presumes, on the contrary, that a man's ego is psychologically capable of anything that is required of it, that it has unlimited power over the id. This is an error; even in normal people the power of controlling the id cannot be increased beyond certain limits. If one asks more of them one produces revolt or neurosis in individuals and makes them unhappy. The command to love the neighbour as ourselves is the strongest defence there is against human agressiveness and it is a superlative example of the unpsychological attitude of the cultural super-ego. The command is impossible to fulfil; such an enormous inflation of the ego can only lower its value and not remedy its evil."[1] This is a perfectly valid protest against a too moralistic and optimistic love perfectionism. But it fails to meet the insights of a religion which knows that the law of love is an impossible possibility and knows how to confess, "There is a law in my members which wars against the law that is in my mind." Freud's strongest defence against human aggressiveness" is incidentally, the revelation of a certain equivocation in his thought. The impossible command is admitted to be a necessity, even though a dangerous one. It would be regarded as less dangerous by Freud if he knew enough about the true genius of prophetic religion to realize that it has resources for relaxing moral tension as well as for creating it.

If the relevance of the love commandment must be asserted against both Christian orthodoxy and against certain types of naturalism, the impossibility of the ideal must be insisted upon against all those forms of naturalism, liberalism, and radicalism which generate utopian illusions and regard the love commandment as ultimately realizable because history knows no limits of its progressive approximations. While modern culture since the eighteenth century has been particularly fruitful of these illusions,

---

[1] Freud, *Civilization and its Discontents*, pp. 139-140.

the logic which underlies them was stated as early as the fourth century of the Christian faith by Pelagius in his controversy with Augustine. He said:

> We contradict the Lord to his face when we say: It is hard, it is difficult; we cannot, we are men; we are encompassed with fragile flesh. O blind madness! O unholy audacity! We charge the God of all knowledge with a two-fold ignorance, that he does not seem to know what he has made nor what he has commanded, as though forgetting the human weakness of which he is himself the author, He imposed laws upon man which he cannot endure.[1]

There is a certain plausibility in the logic of these words, but unfortunately, the facts of human history and the experience of every soul contradict them. The faith which regards the love commandment as a simple possibility rather than an impossible possibility is rooted in a faulty analysis of human nature which fails to understand that though man always stands under infinite possibilities and is potentially related to the totality of existence, he is, nevertheless, and will remain, a creature of finiteness. No matter how much his rationality is refined, he will always see the total situation in which he is involved only from a limited perspective; he will never be able to divorce his reason from its organic relation with the natural impulse of survival with which nature has endowed him; and he will never be able to escape the sin of accentuating his natural will-to-live into an imperial will-to-power by the very protest which his yearning for the eternal tempts him to make against his finiteness.

There is thus a mystery of evil in human life to which modern culture has been completely oblivious. Liberal Christianity, particularly in America, having borrowed heavily from the optimistic credo of modern thought, sought to read this optimism back into the gospels. It was aided in doing this by the fortuitous circumstance that the impossibility of an impossible possibility was implicit rather than explicit in the thought of Jesus. It became explicit only in the theology of Paul. Modern Christianity could thus make the "rediscovery of Jesus" the symbol and basis of its new optimism. The transcendent character of the love ideal was

---

[1] Quoted by N. P. Williams, *op. cit.*, p. 342.

covert rather than overt in the words of Jesus because of the eschatological mould in which it was cast. Jesus thus made demands upon the human spirit, which no finite man can fulfil, without explicitly admitting this situation. This enabled modern liberalism to interpret the words of Jesus in terms of pure optimism.[1] The interpretation of Jesus' own life and character was also brought into conformity with this optimism. For liberal Christianity Christ is the ideal man, whom all men can emulate, once the persuasive charm of his life has captivated their souls. In Christian theology, at its best, the revelation of Christ, the God-man, is a revelation of the paradoxical relation of the eternal to history, which it is the genius of mythical-prophetic religion to emphasize. Christ is thus the revelation of the very impossible possibility which the Sermon on the Mount elaborates in ethical terms. If Christian orthodoxy sometimes tends to resolve this paradox by the picture of a Christ who has been stripped of all qualities which relate him to man and history, Christian liberalism resolves it by reducing Christ to a figure of heroic love who reveals the full possibilities of human nature to us. In either case the total human situation which the mythos of the Christ and the Cross illumines, is obscured. Modern liberalism significantly substitutes the name of "Jesus" for that of "Christ" in most of the sentimental and moralistic exhortations by which it encourages men to "follow in his steps." The relation of the Christ of Christian faith to the Jesus of history cannot be discussed within the confines of this treatise in terms adequate enough to escape misunderstanding. Perhaps it is sufficient to say that the Jesus of history actually created the Christ of faith in the life of the early church, and that his historic life is related to the transcendent Christ as a final and ultimate symbol of a relation which prophetic religion sees between all life and history and the transcendent. In genuine prophetic Christianity the moral qualities of the Christ are not only our hope, but our despair. Out of that despair arises a new hope centred in the revelation of God in Christ. In such faith Christ and the Cross reveal not only the possibilities but the limits

---

[1] Typical statements of this liberal interpretation of gospel ethics may be found, *inter alia*, in Shailer Matthews, *The Gospel and the Modern Man*, and in Francis Peabody's *Jesus Christ and the Social Question*.

of human finitude in order that a more ultimate hope may arise
from the contrite recognition of those limits. Christian faith is, in
other words, a type of optimism which places its ultimate
confidence in the love of God and not the love of man, in the
ultimate and transcendent unity of reality and not in tentative and
superficial harmonies of existence which human ingenuity may
contrive. It insists, quite logically, that this ultimate hope becomes possible only to those who no longer place their confidence
in purely human possibilities. Repentance is thus the gateway into
the Kingdom of God.

The real crux of the issue between essential Christianity and
modern culture lies at this point. The conflict is between those
who have a confidence in human virtue which human nature
cannot support and those who have looked too deeply into life and
their own souls to place their trust in so broken a reed. It is out of
such despair, "the godly sorrow which worketh repentance," that
faith arises. The conflict lies here and not between modern science
and discredited myth, though it has been complicated by the
metaphysical pretensions of science and the scientific pretensions
of religious myth. Naturally in such a conflict the vicissitudes of
history may determine the tentative victories of one side or the
other. Thus modern naturalism, which imagines itself rooted in
the achievements of science, is really the fruit of a period of history
in which technical achievement and an expanding capitalism gave
a momentary plausibility to the hope that human reason could
create a universal social harmony in the world. It made the hope
plausible at least to those classes in society who did not suffer from
the cruelties of a capitalistic civilization. The utopianism of
liberalism has run its course, but the utopianism of naturalism in
general will not be spent until it is proved that the civilization
which the proletarian rebels against a bourgeois civilization will
build, will not achieve the perfect justice which they expect. A
Christian-prophetic interpretation of life is at a disadvantage in
periods when the total dimensions of life are obscured by specific
perils and immediate possibilities. Sometimes it increases the
disadvantage under which it labours by failing to relate its total
view redemptively to the urgent issues which men face in the crisis
of history. In such crisis outraged nature inevitably seeks the
anodyne of illusory hopes; but the tendency is accentuated when a

profound religion insulates its profundities so that they have no
relevance to immediate situations.

While the vicissitudes of history thus determine the time and
season when illusions wax and wane, it is not impossible to
discover the fallacies which underly them, and thus to guard
against them even when their time is ripe. The whole of human
history reveals to what degree human finiteness and sin enter into
all human actions and attitudes. The Marxian theory of economic
determinism calls attention to a quality of man's spirituality which
liberal culture had overlooked and which even historic religion
had forgotten. It reveals itself in all moral aspirations and cultural
achievements. No matter what the pretensions, moral and religious ideals, legal codes and cultural attainments are never developed in an historical and social vacuum. The supposedly
objective and dispassionate ideas of the world of culture proceed
from particular perspectives, and are determined by the social
locus of the observer. They are informed by all the natural
passions which exist side by side in the same psyche with the
capacity of rationality, and they are always subject to the
corruption of man's spiritual pretension, to human sin, in short.
The Marxian emphasis upon the means of production as the actual
basis of spiritual achievements and pretensions is right in so far as
it regards the necessities of physical existence as the most primary
influences upon human ideas. Its error lies in the artificial limits
which it places upon human finiteness. Not only a ruling class but
a ruling nation, and a ruling oligarchy within a class, and the
rebellious leadership of a subject class, and a functional group
within a class, and a racial minority or majority within a
functional group; all these and many more are bound to judge a
total human problem from their own particular perspective. It is
probably true that the combination of the finiteness of reason and
the dishonesty of the human heart expresses itself with peculiarly
demonic force in the class conflicts of modern civilization. But it is
not isolated there. There is no human situation, not even the most
individual relationship, whether in a crassly unjust society or in
one which has achieved a modicum of justice, in which it does not
reveal itself. The insights into human nature which Marxism has
fortunately added to modern culture belong to the forgotten
insights of prophetic religion. They must be reappropriated with

gratitude for their rediscovery. But since prophetic religion must deal with the total human situation it cannot accept them merely as weapons in one particular social conflict. To do so would mean to make them the basis of new spiritual pretensions. The pathos of Marxian spirituality is that it sees the qualified and determined character of all types of spirituality except its own. Thus the recognition of human finiteness becomes the basis of a new type of pretension that finiteness has been transcended.

Human finiteness and sin are revealed with particular force in collective relationships; but they are present in even the most individual and personal relationships. Individuals within the bounds of a particular community have a threefold advantage over collective organisms. The judgments by which they relate their life to other life proceeds from common presuppositions and they are therefore in less danger of condemning others by standards of judgment which have emerged from, and are applicable to, only their own situation. They have a greater capacity for self-transcendence than communities; and finally the more intimate contacts of a community allow an interpenetration of life with life not possible in collective relationships. But all these advantages are in terms of degree and not of kind. Our better self, the self of consistent purposes, may judge our worser self, the self enslaved by momentary passions; but the self-transcendence remains incomplete. We always judge ourselves by our own standards and weigh ourselves in balances which give us a special advantage. Hence the validity of St Paul's judgment: "I know nothing against myself; yet am I not hereby justified: but he that judgeth me is the Lord."[1] The common standards of judgment drawn from some common moral tradition, which arbitrate the conflicts between individuals in a given community, are hence more adequate instruments of arbitration and appeasement than the varying standards of different communities. But these common standards are always qualified by the particular perspectives of different families, classes, cultural groups, and social functions. The most terrific social conflicts actually occur in intimate communities in which intensity of social cohesion accentuates the social distance of various groups and individuals. Even in the most

[1] 1 Corinthians iv. 4.

intimate community, the family, parental, conjugal, and filial affection is no perfect guarantee of justice and harmony. All these forces of natural sympathy may become façades behind which the will-to-power operates. Even when it is less pronounced than the imperialism of groups it may be more deadly for operating at such close range.

As previously intimated, the full evil of human finitude and sin is most vividly revealed in conflicts between national communities. While the Marxians are right in insisting that the class interests of dominant economic classes within the nations accentuate these conflicts, there is no evidence that they are prompted only by such interests. They present a tragic revelation of the impossibility of the law of love because no party to the conflict has a perspective high enough to judge the merits of the opponent's position. Every appeal to moral standards thus degenerates into a moral justification of the self against the enemy. Parties to a dispute inevitably make themselves judges over it and thus fall into the sin of pretending to be God.

Any one of the contemporary international tensions may illustrate the point. The rivalry between Jews and Arabs in Palestine is a conflict between two races and religions, involving not only the natural will-to-live of two collective racial organisms, but the economic differences between the feudalism of the Arabs and the technical civilization which the Jews are able to introduce into Palestine. How can a high enough rational and moral perspective be found to arbitrate the issue between them? How is the ancient and hereditary title of the Jew to Palestine to be measured against the right of the Arab's present possession? Or how is one to judge the relative merits of modern Jewish against ancient Moslem culture without introducing criteria which are involved in and do not transcend the struggle? The participants cannot find a common ground of rational morality from which to arbitrate the issues because the moral judgments which each brings to them are formed by the very historical forces which are in conflict. Such conflicts are therefore sub- and supra-moral. The effort to bring such a conflict under the dominion of a spiritual unity may be partly successful, but it always produces a tragic by-product of the spiritual accentuation of natural conflict. The introduction of religious motives into these conflicts is usually no more than the final and most demonic pretension. Religion may be regarded as the last and final effort of the human spirit to escape relativity and gain a vantagepoint in the eternal. But when this effort is made without a contrite recognition of the finiteness and relativity which characterizes human spirituality, even in its moments of yearning for the transcendent, religious aspiration is transmuted into sinful dishonesty. Historic religions, which crown the structure of historic cultures, thus become the most brutal weapons in the conflict between the cultures.

The conflict between Arab and Jew was finally arbitrated by the British Empire. But Britain was not an impartial judge in the dispute since imperial interests were at stake in it. It would be more accurate to record, therefore, that the struggle between these two social wills was suppressed by a third and stronger social will, that of the British Empire.

The contemporary struggle between France and Germany is an elementary conflict between two national wills, destined by geography and history to contend for the hegemony of the Continent. A transcendent perspective upon the issues at stake is impossible not only for the disputants, but even for the so-called impartial observers. By what standard is one to measure their conflicting claims? How is one to apportion relative blame upon the hysteria of Germany and the fear complex of France? Both are examples of pathological behaviour and such behaviour is not easily brought under the scrutiny of moral criteria. If one were to decide that Germany is more demented than France one would also have to note that Germany was most recently defeated in a World War and practically imprisoned by its victors. Beating a national head against prison bars is hardly conducive to sanity, particularly not if the jailer is relentless and vindictive and tries to hide these passions behind a pious smirk and his concern for "international justice" and the "peace of Europe." But how, on the other hand, can one blame France for fearing a nation numerically fifty per cent stronger than she or for seeking to preserve the fruits of a victory gained by the help of allies who are not certain to make common cause against the enemy in the next instance? One might come to the conclusion that France has unwisely aggravated the belligerency of her foe and created by her fears the kind of Germany deserving to be feared. But to see that is not to see a way out. It is merely to see the whole tragedy of the human situation in miniature. National animosities might be appeased if nations could hear the accusing word, "Let him who is without sin cast the first stone." Only a forgiving love, grounded in repentance, is adequate to heal the animosities between nations. But that degree of love is an impossibility for nations. It is a very rare achievement among individuals; and the mind and heart of collective man is notoriously less imaginative than that of the individual.

It must be admitted, of course, that international conflicts are arbitrated and mitigated to a certain degree by the force of the international community. But the League of Nations, which was expected to provide the inchoate international community with genuine organs of international cohesion, is significantly disintegrating, because its organs of cohesion were nothing more than the wills of the strong nations which compose it; and none of these nations are capable of an international perspective transcending their own interests. Russia has been drawn into the League merely as a way of forming an alliance with France against Germany. England, though genuinely devoted to the League, has sabotaged it from the French perspective by a separate naval agreement with Germany, prompted, in her own opinion, by the desire to win Germany to peace by conciliation and fairness, and prompted in French opinion by the traditional English policy of the balance of power on the Continent.

In a similar fashion the imperial interests of France and England prevented League action against Japan's adventure in Manchuria. America was properly scornful at the time of the impotence of the League against Japan and therefore took the place of the faltering League as the conscience of mankind toward Japan. Only it was difficult for America to remember that a conflict between American and Japanese imperial interests in China was a more potent cause of our concern over Japanese aggression than abstract conceptions of international justice. All of the moral judgments which peaceful nations pass upon the nations which threaten the peace, principally Japan, Germany, and Italy, are, significantly, the judgments of secure and powerful nations against those less secure and more tardy in initiating their imperial enterprises.

There is, in short, no position in an international conflict from which impartial judgments are possible. Every judgment is coloured by interest and every claim to impartiality fails in the end to obscure the partial and particular interests which prompted or corrupted it. Thus the international situation is a perfect picture of human finitude and a tragic revelation of the consequences of sinful dishonesty which accompany every effort to transcend it.

An analysis of the class conflicts of modern society merely increases the evidence of human finiteness, already established in the survey of individual and national actions. But it also, suggests one needed qualification. In the struggle between property-owners and workers, broadly considered, between the rich and poor, which agitates every modern industrial nation, certain moral judgments are possible which are less under the peril of demonic pretension and sinful dishonesty than either individual or national judgments, being less subjective than the former and less dependent upon the relativities of national cultures than the latter. They stand under the criterion of the simplest of all moral principles, that of equal justice. That principle has been operative in all the advances made by human society and its application to the modern social situation is obviously valid. In a struggle between those who enjoy inordinate privileges and those who lack the basic essentials of the good life it is fairly clear that a religion which holds love to be the final law of life stultifies itself if it does not support equal justice as a political and economic approxima-tion of the ideal of love. This matter will be dealt with more fully in later chapters. It is mentioned here only to call attention to the fact that the relativity of all moral ideals cannot absolve us of the necessity and duty of choosing between relative values; and that the choice is sometimes so clear as to become an imperative one. The moral issues underlying the social struggle in industrial civilization are, in a sense, merely typical of a whole range of moral and social problems in which moral judgment is fairly clear and social action imperative.

Nevertheless, the struggle between classes is not free of the sins of dishonesty and pretension which flow from human finiteness. Here too it is necessary to insist that the law of love is an impossibility for finite men and that failure to recognize this fact results in an accentuation of the conflict.

The class wars of modernity are something of a triangular struggle between three classes, the landed aristocrats, the merchants, and the workers. The victories of democracy in the eighteenth and nineteenth centuries were triumphs of an alliance of merchants and workers over the aristocrats who defended their position behind the bulwarks of feudalism and monarchy. The contemporary struggle is between the workers on the one hand and an alliance of aristocrats and merchants on the other. The merchants have shifted their alliance from the workers to the aristocrats because their common interests as property-owners with the landed gentry are more important to them now than their erstwhile common interest with the workers in democracy. This shift of allegiance on the part of the merchants proves to what degree democracy was an instrument of bourgeois class interest for them. It was used to establish both their political and their economic power against the power of landed wealth which controlled the feudal and monarchial political forms. The intricacies of this triangular struggle are not relevant to our thesis, except perhaps as they reveal to what degree such universal values as democracy were used as façades of class interest. What is important and relevant at this point is the fact that each one of these classes had and has its own particular method for claiming absolute and ultimate significance for the particular and relative interests of its class. Traditional religion, particularly Catholicism, was used and abused by the feudal aristocracy to place its enemies at a disadvantage. Its relative justice pretended to be a "divine justice," and its governments claimed to be divinely ordained. The civilization and culture of the merchants used Protestantism in something of the same fashion as feudalism appropriated the spiritual authority of Catholicism. But the real priest of the bourgeois civilization was the scientist and the liberal idealist who proved that the necessities of a commercial civilization were in accord with the eternal principles of morality and rationality. The real religion of a commercial civilization is liberal culture. The confidence of this culture in the ability of reason and the scientific method of achieving impartial and "objective" value judgments results in exactly the same kind of spiritual sanctification of class interests as is achieved by an uncritical religion. Thus the simple faith of modern culture in the impartiality of human reason became a religion by which a commercial civilization could claim ultimate significance for all of its relative moral and social ideals: liberty, property, democracy, *laissez-faire* economics, etc. The scientists have, of course, not been the witting, but rather the unwitting, tools of class interest. Perhaps it would be better to say that the proportion of personally honest scientists to those who have consciously weighed scientific opinion in the interest of a class would probably be in a ratio similar to that between honest and dishonest priests of the medieval Church.

Modern radical social philosophy, championing the cause of the workers against both aristocrats and plutocrats, properly pours its contempt upon the scientific "objectivists." It knows very well that every social theory and every social value judgment proceeds from a particular locus and is informed by a particular economic and social interest. That insight is, in fact, its great contribution to social thought. But it finds a new way of satisfying the sinful desire of finite man to be more finite. It declares that the relative position of the proletariat is really an absolute one, that the victory of the workers is automatically a victory for the whole of society, and that the civilization to be built by them will be a utopia in which everyone will give according to his ability and take according to his need, that is, the law of love will be perfectly fulfilled.

There is no reason to suppose that this demonic element in communism will be any less dangerous than the moral and spiritual pretensions of either the aristocrats or the merchants. The cruelty of Russian communists toward their "class enemies," their naïve identification of every form of human egoism with the "capitalistic spirit," and their foolish hope that the liquidation of an unjust class will solve every problem of justice, all prove that here again the social problem is complicated rather than solved when finite men make a final effort to transcend their finiteness and set themselves up as unqualified arbiters over the issues of life. The problem of achieving a just society in the Western World is being needlessly complicated by a social philosophy which tempts the rebels against social injustice to an intransigence and dogmatism inconsistent with the necessities of a wise statesmanship and prevents them from working in alliance with other victims of injustice, whose view upon life is different from their own (the agrarians, for instance).

There is, in short, no problem of history and no point in society from which one may not observe that the same man who touches the fringes of the infinite in his moral life remains imbedded in finiteness, that he increases the evil in his life if he tries to overcome it without regard to his limitations. Therefore it is as important to know what is impossible as what is possible in the moral demands under which all human beings stand.

5

THE LAW OF LOVE
IN POLITICS AND ECONOMICS
Criticism of Christian Orthodoxy

The field of politics and economics is a particularly strategic testing-ground of the adequacy and relevance of a religio-moral world view. Its realities betray the impossibility of an ultimate ideal more vividly than the realm of personal moral relationships. At the same time its necessities are concerned with the life and death, the happiness and misery, of the multitudes; and its qualified achievements and tentative harmonies and unities may, in spite of their tentative and qualified character, become the important symbols and harbingers of a more ultimate and absolute unity of life.

The importance of the political and economic problem increases in every decade of modern existence because a technical civilization has so accentuated the intensity and extent of social cohesion that human happiness depends increasingly upon a just organization and adjustment of the political and economic mechanisms by which the common life of man is ordered. Even though it may be true that the human spirit faces ultimate problems which transcend the relationship of man to his society, and that all solutions of the social problem are more tentative and less final from the perspective of a profound religion than the advocates of specific social panaceas realize, a socially imperilled generation will have both the inclination and the right to dismiss profound and ultimate interpretations of life which are not made relevant to the immediate problems of social justice. Men whose very existence is imperilled and whose universe of meaning is reduced to chaos by the social maladjustments of a technical society may be pardoned if they dismiss, as a luxury which they cannot afford, any "profound" religion which does not concern itself with these problems.

The problem of politics and economics is the problem of justice. The question of politics is how to coerce the anarchy of conflicting human interests into some kind of order, offering human beings the greatest possible opportunity for mutual support. In the field of collective behaviour the force of egoistic passion is so strong that the only harmonies possible are those which manage to neutralize this force through balances of power, through mutual defences against its inordinate expression, and through techniques for harnessing its energy to social ends. All these possibilities represent something less than the ideal of love. Yet the law of love is involved in all approximations of justice, not only as the source of the norms of justice, but as an ultimate perspective by which their limitations are discovered.

Unfortunately, the relation of Christianity to the problems of politics and economics has not been a particularly fortunate or inspiring one. Christianity has been more frequently a source of confusion in political and social ethics than a source of insight and constructive guidance. Such an indictment could not be sustained unqualifiedly, of course. The contribution of Thomasian Catholicism to the peace and order of thirteenth-century Europe and the dynamic relation of Calvinism to the democratic developments of the seventeenth and eighteenth century are obvious exceptions to the indictment. Others equally significant might be mentioned. Yet on the whole it must be admitted that rationalistic political theory from Aristotle and the Stoics to the thought of the eighteenth century and the theories of Marx, have contributed more to a progressive reassessment of the problems of justice with which politics deals than either orthodox or the liberal Christian thought. Among the many possible causes of this failure of Christianity in politics the most basic is the tendency of Christianity to destroy the dialectic of prophetic religion, either by sacrificing time and history to eternity or by giving ultimate significance to the relativities of history. Christian orthodoxy chose the first alternative, and Christian liberalism the second. The problems of politics were confused by the undue pessimism of the orthodox Church and the undue sentimentality of the liberal Church. In the one case the fact of the "sinfulness of the world" was used as an excuse for the complacent acceptance of whatever imperfect justice a given social order had established. The fear of the possible disintegration of a sinful world into anarchy prompted a rather frantic and pious commendation of whatever order had been historically established. In the other case the problems of politics were approached from the perspective of a sentimental moralism and with no understanding for either the mechanistic and amoral factors in social life or the mechanical and technical prerequisites of social justice.

No doubt economic determinism can throw some light upon the tragic failure of both orthodox and liberal Churches in the field of politics. If Christian perfectionism on the one hand and Christian realism on the other have both been used to thwart the efforts at a higher justice in society, the suspicion naturally arises that the same use to which these opposite doctrines are put is determined not by the doctrines themselves, but by the similar social interests of the people who profess them. The Christian Churches in both the Middle Ages and the modern period were comprised, on the whole, of the classes which dominated their social orders. Their ability to use diametrically opposite religious tendencies as grist for the mills of their class interests proves that no element in human culture, not even the final religious effort to transcend the relativity of culture, can escape the fate of becoming, and being used as, an instrument of relative and partial social interests. Yet the Christian Church has never been purely the tool of particular social classes; and it could be maintained with equal validity that no cultural or spiritual enterprise of the human spirit can be explained purely in terms of the special social circumstances which condition and corrupt it. The very fact that an acute analysis of conditioning circumstances always involves and implies a charge of corruption suggests that there is any inner core of integrity and truth which can be corrupted. It is impossible to tell an effective lie without availing oneself of an element of truth. A pure lie is self-defeating. It is equally impossible to make use of spiritual forces for the defence and advancement of particular interests if they do not contain some values which transcend those interests.

The failure of the Christian Church in politics can, therefore, not be explained purely in terms of the economic and social interests which drove the historic Church into a position of social conservatism. The source must be sought in the character and nature of historic Christianity itself. It will be found in the fact that a religious interpretation of life, which does justice to the ultimate problems of human existence and is able to apprehend the final possibilities of good and evil, does not find it easy to deal with the questions of relative good and evil, which are the very stuff of the political order. Liberal Christianity adopted the simple expedient of denying, in effect, the reality of evil in order to maintain its hope in the triumph of the ideal of love in the world. This results in political theories which are not able to cope with the problem of establishing a relative justice in society through the strategic use of coercion, conflict, and balances of power. Orthodox Christianity was so well aware of the fact of sin that it saw in the ideal of love only an ultimate criterion by which all human social achievments are revealed in their imperfections. This is indeed a proper function of the law of love in any religion which appreciates the transcendent character of the ultimate ideal. But Christian orthodoxy failed to derive any significant politico-moral principles from the law of love. It did not realize that the law of love is not only in position of ultimate transcendence over all moral achievements, but that it suggests possibilities which immediately transcend any achievements of justice by which society has integrated its life. It therefore destroyed a dynamic relationship between the ideal of love and the principles of justice. The social principles of orthodox Christianity have, consequently, been determined by ideals of justice which were informed by reverence for the principle of order rather than by the attraction of the ideal of love.

The political ideas which governed Christian orthodoxy's strategy of compromise with the necessities of politics are chiefly drawn from two sources, the Pauline conception of the divine ordinance of government (Rom. xiii) and the Stoic conception of the natural law. The natural law is, according to both Stoic

teachers and the Christian fathers, the law of reason. It supposedly establishes universal standards of right conduct and
action which are not identical with the standards of love but have
equal validity as laws of God. The theory of the natural law is thus
the instrument by which the orthodox Church adjusted itself to
the world after the hope of the *parousia* waned. This was natural
enough since the love perfectionism of the gospels, with its
implied anarchism and universalism, was obviously not applicable to the arbitration of conflicting interests and the choice of
relative values required in an imperfect world. The development
of natural law theories in Christianity has been criticized as an
apostasy from the Christian ideal of love. But all such criticisms
are informed by a moral sentimentalism which does not recognize
to what degree all decent human actions, even when under the
tension and inspiration of the love commandment, are in fact
determined by rational principles of equity and justice, by law
rather than by love.

The difficulty in the Christian application of the theory of
natural law lies elsewhere. It is to be found in the undue emphasis
placed upon the relative natural law which was applicable to the
world of sin, as against the absolute natural law which demanded
equality and freedom. This distinction between two kinds of
natural law was also inherited from Stoicism. Sometimes it was
expressed in terms of a distinction between the *jus naturale* and the
jus gentium, the former embodying the absolute demands of
equality and freedom and the latter regulating the government,
coercion, conflict, and slavery existing in the historic institutions
of society. The significant development in the Christian adoption
of this distinction lay in the particular emphasis placed by
Christian orthodoxy upon the requirements of the *jus gentium* as
necessities of the world of sin.[1] The deeper pessimism of Christian
orthodoxy is revealed in this emphasis. As a consequence the
Christian Church could insist in the same breath on the freedom
and equality of all men before God and on the rightfulness of
slavery as God's way of punishing and controlling a sinful world.
The principle of equality was thereby robbed of its regulative

---

[1] A full analysis of this development of Christian thought may be found in A. J. Carlyle's
Medieval Political Theory in the West.

function in the development of the principles of justice. It was relegated to a position of complete transcendence with the ideal of love. The consequence was an attitude of complacency toward whatever injustices in the economic and political order had become historically established. This continues to be the baneful influence of orthodox Christianity upon political questions to this day. It cannot be denied that the belief in an ultimate equality and freedom of all souls before God did frequently encourage the Church to qualify the attitude toward slavery in the ancient world. Above all, it sometimes led to a higher ethic in the Christian communion than in the political state. But it must also be noted that the Church usually capitulated in the end to the lower standards which it failed to challenge in the state.

If any problem of human justice is examined carefully it will be discovered that some such distinction as is suggested in the two types of natural law is as justified as it is unjustified to make the distinction as unqualifiedly and absolutely as has been the case in Christian thought. In every human situation and relationship there is an ideal possibility and there are given facts of human nature, historic and fortuitous inequalities, geographic and other natural divisive forces, contingent and accidental circumstances. The ideal possibility for men involved in any social situation may always be defined in terms of freedom and equality. Their highest good consists in freedom to develop the essential potentialities of their nature without hindrance. There can be no development of personality without discipline; but the ideal discipline is self-imposed, or at least not imposed by agents who have other motives than the enhancement of the ultimate values of human life. Since human beings live in a society in which other human beings are competing with them for the opportunity of a fuller development of life, the next highest good is equality; for there is no final principle of arbitration between conflicting human interests except that which equates the worth of competing individuals. If their actual worth is not equal, there is always the possibility that their potential worth is; and that the potential equality is hindered from realizing itself only by the accidental or hereditary advantages of one person over another.

A rational analysis reveals both the ideal possibility and the actual situation from which one must begin. In that sense there are really two natural laws—that which reason commands ultimately and the compromise which reason makes with the contingent and arbitrary forces of human existence. The ideal possibility is really an impossibility, a fact to which both Stoic and Christian doctrine do justice by the myth of the Golden Age in Stoic doctrine and of the age of perfection before the Fall in Christian doctrine. The ideal is an impossibility because both the contingencies of nature and the sin in the human heart prevent men from ever living in that perfect freedom and equality which the whole logic of the moral life demands. The ideal equality will be relativized, as has been previously observed, not only by the fortuitous circumstances of nature and history, but by the necessities of social cohesion and organic social life, which will give some men privileges and powers which other men lack; and finally by human sin, for it is inevitable that men should take advantage of privileges with which nature or necessity has endowed them and should enhance them beyond the limits of the one and the requirements of the other.

Yet this impossibility is not one which can be relegated simply to the world of transcendence. It offers immediate possibilities of a higher good in every given situation. We may never realize equality, but we cannot accept the inequalities of capitalism or any other unjust social system complacently. There is no equality between the sexes, nature having placed a greater biological restraint upon the freedom of a woman than upon man. Yet the more advanced societies have properly sought to circumvent nature in diminishing the disabilities from which women suffer in the development of talents which transcend their maternal function. Nor can any intelligent society accept inequalities in ability between classes or races as final. They may be, and usually are, caused by forces of nature and history which an intelligent control of social life can greatly restrict and sometimes completely overcome.

The principles of equal justice are thus approximations of the law of love in the kind of imperfect world which we know and not principles which belong to a world of transcendent perfection. Equality has no place in such a perfect world because this principle of equality presupposes competition of life with life and seeks to prevent this competition from resulting in exploitation, by advancing and defending the claims and interests of one life with equal force against every other life. Since the law of love demands that all life be affirmed, the principle that all conflicting claims of life be equally affirmed is a logical approximation of the law of love in a world in which conflict is inevitable.

The ideal of love and the ideal of equality therefore stand in an ascending scale of transcendence to the facts of existence. The ideal of equality is a part of the natural law which transcends existence, but is more immediately relevant to social and economic problems because it is an ideal law, and as law presupposes a recalcitrant nature which must be brought into submission to it. The ideal of love, on the other hand, transcends all law. It knows nothing of the recalcitrance of nature in historical existence. It is the fulfilment of the law. It is impossible to construct a social ethic out of the ideal of love in its pure form, because the ideal presupposes the resolution of the conflict of life with life, which it is the concern of law to mitigate and restrain. For this reason Christianity really had no social ethic until it appropriated the Stoic ethic. As the ideal of love must relate itself to the problems of a world in which its perfect realization is not possible, the most logical modification and application of the ideal in a world in which life is in conflict with life is the principle of equality which strives for an equilibrium in the conflict.

The failure of Christian orthodoxy to relate the principle of equality to the law of love on the one hand and to the problems of relative justice on the other, resulted in a constant temptation to a complacent acceptance of historic forms of relative justice which ought to have been regarded, and by later ages were regarded, as injustice. A perfectionist ethic thus had the tragic consequence of increasing complacency toward remediable imperfections in justice. The force of this pessimism was accentuated by another element in Christian faith: the force of pious gratitude for the goodness of life and creation. The influence of this piety toward the natural world operated to increase Christian complacency toward the established, given, and traditional modes of social organization. Since there were rich and poor, God must have intended the distinction to exist, for nothing exists without God, in the thought of the Christian Church. This motive in Christian theology frequently reduces Christian ethics to a pantheistic diminution of the ethical element in life. Whenever the prophetic faith that all things have their source in God is not balanced by the other article of prophetic faith, that all things have their fulfilment in God, ethical tension is destroyed and the result is similar to a pantheistic religious acceptance of life as it is. It is significant that the amalgamation of nationalistic paganism and Christian faith attempted by the Nazi movement in the German Evangelical Church avails itself of the idea of God's creation of the natural differences of race and blood for the purpose of giving a religious sanctification to the cult of race. Thus one of the Nazi theologians writes: "If blood deteriorates, then spirit is also destroyed. The blood brotherhood of our people was deteriorating. It was possible for the Church, through her belief in the order of creation *(Schoepfungsordnung)*, to appreciate the mystery of the strength and character derived from blood as holy."[1] Or again, "The people, the race, is a creation of God. God wishes mankind to live in the division of nations." The ability of Christian theology to regard the contingent and historically relative facts of human existence as both the immutable characteristics of a sinful world and yet also as divinely ordained and created values is due to an interesting and baneful perversion of the prophetic paradoxical estimate of the world as both evil and good, as being the creation of God and yet standing under divine judgment. Since the religious appreciation of the world and the religious criticism of the world are not used as sources of discrimination between the good and evil in specific instances, the consequence is merely a completely immoral compound of religious optimism and religious pessimism.

It must be admitted that the Lutheran doctrine of the *Schoepfungsordnung* is not a valueless concept. It is a symbol of the religio-mythical understanding for the organic aspects of life which rationalistic morality frequently fails to appreciate. Both liberal and radical social morality inclines to regard the organic unities of family, race, and nation as irrational idiosyncrasies which a more perfect rationality will destroy. So an English communist writes: "It must not be considered that communists consider the existence of separate national cultures, separate languages, and the like, will be features of a fully developed world

---

[1] E. Hirsch, *Das Kirchliche Wollen der Deutschen Christen.*

communism. Such phenomena belong to the present, not to the ultimate stage of human development. It is clear that man will in the end tire of the inconvenient idiosyncrasies of locality and will wish to pool the cultural heritage of the human race into a world synthesis."[1] It would be difficult to find a more perfect and naïve expression of the modern illusion that human reason will be able to become the complete master of all the contingent, irrational, and illogical forces of the natural world which underlie and condition all human culture.

The frantic and morbid emphasis upon national and racial solidarities in modern reactionary politics is undoubtedly a device of the imperiled oligarchies of the modern world to obscure the issues of the class struggle. But is is a device which succeeds so well only because the advocates of a just social order have not taken sufficient account of the perennial force and the qualified virtue of the more organic and less rational human relationships. Nature, history, and traditions create communities and establish loyalties and sentiments which are bound to be in conflict with the more rational and inclusive communities and loyalties which human reason can project. Since these narrower loyalties result in conflict and anarchy, they must be constantly subjected to criticism. Without this criticism the harmless divisions and disharmonies of nature are heightened into insufferable proportions by human sin. But they cannot be eliminated; and the effort to do so merely results in desperate and demonic affirmations of the imperiled values inherent in them. From the standpoint of certain rational and spiritual aspirations of the human spirit the differences between the sexes are irrational and illogical. Biological facts have determined motherhood to be a more absorbing vocation than the avocation of fatherhood, and thereby inhibited a mother's freedom in developing certain talents which are irrelevant to the maternal function. An adequate social morality will neither exclude women from the professions because of this fact, nor yet quarrel with nature to the extent of imperiling the responsibilities of motherhood. It will be guided, in other words, both by the principles of equality and by the organic facts of existence. Such an attitude toward differences of sex may be

---

[1] John Strachey, *The Coming Struggle for Power*, p. 389.

taken as typical of the moral necessities in all situations in which the forces of nature are in conflict with the imperatives of man as spirit.

If the forces of optimism and pessimism are compounded in the orthodox Christian attitude toward the organic aspects of life, they are united in an even more baneful mixture in its attitude toward government. Government is too obviously the construct of human history to be regarded simply as a part of the *Schoepfungsordnung*, the order of creation. It therefore receives a special sanctification as an ordinance of God. The emphasis upon government as a divine ordinance in orthodox thought is not only derived from the general theory of the natural law, which does, indeed, support it, but rests particularly upon the words of St Paul: "Let every soul be subject unto the higher powers. For there is no power but of God; the powers that be are ordained of God. Whosoever, therefore, resisteth the powers, resisteth the ordinance of God—for rulers are not a terror to good works, but to the evil. . . ."[1] No passage of Scripture has had so fateful an influence upon Christian political thought as this word. If it is compared with the words of Jesus, "The kings of the Gentiles exercise lordship over them; and they that exercise authority upon them are called benefactors. But ye shall not be so; but he that is greatest among you, let him be as the younger; and he that is chief as he that doth serve,"[2] one may observe a significant difference between the critical attitude of a prophetic religion toward the perils of power and the uncritical acceptance of the virtues of social power in a less prophetic type of religious thought.

The theory of the divine ordinance of government was partially derived from Christian pessimism in the sense that government was justified as an instrument of God to prevent the world from falling into anarchy. "Since men hated their fellow-men," said Irenæus, one of the early Fathers, "and fell into confusion of every kind, God set some men over each other, imposing the fear of man upon man." This argument is logical enough. Coercion is a necessity of social cohesion, and coercion demands the concentration of power in government and the manipulation of that power

---

[1] Romans xiii. 1.
[2] Luke xxii. 25.

by some authority. In the same spirit St Isidore of Seville regards both government and slavery as a consequence of and remedy for sin. The difficulty in Christian thought is that piety unduly accentuates the virtue of government by regarding it as unqualifiedly the fruit of God's power. Thus the pessimistic note derived from the emphasis upon the sinfulness of the world unduly accentuates the possibilities of anarchy, which government checks, while the pious note adds the aura of sanctity to the virtue of government.

Both elements are still influential in orthodox Christian thought. The pessimistic motive, and the conservative, not to say reactionary, consequences which flow from it are very marked in modern German theology, including that of the dialectical school. Emil Brunner writes: "The projection of ideal (political) programmes is not only useless, but harmful, because it creates illusions, dissipates moral energy and tempts its proponents to become self-righteous critics of their fellows. The most important consideration for a better social order is that of practical possibility, since the question is one of order and not of ethical ideals. The prophetic demand, which does not concern itself with the possible and the impossible, has, of course, its own relevance as proclamation of the unconditioned law. But it has this significance only if it is presented not as a specific prgramme, but as a general demand—*i.e.*, if it does not involve immediate political realization. When the question is one of immediate and practical problems, the rule must be: The given order is the best as long as a better one cannot be realized immediately and without interruption. . . . The Christian must submit himself to a social order—which is in itself loveless. He must do this if he is not to evade the most urgent of all demands of the love commandment, the demand to protect the dyke which saves human life from chaos."[1] This logic manages not only to express an excessive fear of chaos and to obviate any possibility of a Christian justification of social change by allowing only such change as will create a new order "immediately and without interruption"; but it neatly dismisses the Christian ideal from any immediate relevance to political issues. The same type of logic and the same theory of government

---

[1] Emil Brunner, *Das Gebot und die Ordnungen*, pp. 208-214.

as a dyke against chaos carries Gogarten completely into the political philosophy of fascism.[1] If fascism may be regarded as being informed by a frantic fear of the chaos which might result if an old social order broke down, and as leading to the very anarchy which it fears through its futile attempt to preserve a disintegrated order artificially, after history has dissipated its essential vitality, we might come to the conclusion that fascism is really the unfortunate fruit of Christian pessimism. The theory that government is justified mainly by the negative task of checking chaos is held in common by both fascism and Christian orthodoxy. It may be that the political principles of the former are, at least partially, derived from the latter.

The pious element in orthodox political thought which endows government with an unwarranted aura of sanctity is not as obvious in modern orthodoxy as the pessimistic element. It wrought its worst havoc from the day of Constantine to the rise of modern democracy. In that long period the danger of regarding the mechanisms of power which control society with undue reverence was fully revealed. The idea of the divine right of the ruler, a conception which wedded Christianity to monarchism for centuries, achieved particular prestige in the sixteenth and seventeenth centuries, when nationalism and the politics of the commercial classes used it to defeat the power of the nobles and to substitute national unity for feudal anarchy. But it was implicit in Christian doctrine through all those centuries. Fortunately, the conflict of the Church with the empire qualified the Catholic emphasis upon the divine right of kings, imparting somewhat of a "whig" and quasi-democratic colouring to Catholic political theory. Protestant orthodoxy supported the divine right of rulers more unqualifiedly than did Catholicism, just as it has tended to be more subservient to the nation, for in the latter papal internationalism created a moral fulcrum from which the Church could be critical toward both king and nation. Nevertheless, the total weight of both types of orthodoxy was on the side of whatever ruler had established himself, no matter by what means, since piety regarded his power as derived from God.

The influence of piety upon politics has tended not only to establish an intimate relation between Christianity and

---

[1] F. Gogarten, *Politische Ethik.*

monarchism, but also to support the particular monarch who happened to rule. Both St Augustine and St Isidore of Seville believed in the divine appointment of even wicked rulers, and St Gregory taught the duty of submission to evil rulers. There are always a few critical voices in the history of orthodoxy against this counsel of acquiescence, as that, for instance, of Peter Crassus: "Render unto Cæsar the things that are Cæsar's, but not unto Tiberius the things that are Tiberius'; Cæsar is good, but Tiberius is bad." This word, in which the necessary distinction is made between government as a symbol of the principle of order and particular governments with their inevitable vices, partially anticipates the sentiment of Thomas Paine: "Society is the fruit of our virtues, but government the product of our wickedness."

Nevertheless, such critical voices were the exception rather than the rule in orthodox Christian thought. The idea that evil rulers are meant by God to be a punishment for evil people reinforced the general conservatism and the acquiescence of the Church toward unjust politics. Even Calvin wrote: "Wherefore if we are cruelly vexed by an inhuman prince or robbed and plundered by one avaricious, or left without protection by one negligent, or even if we are inflicted by one sacrilegious and unbelieving, let us first of all remember our offences against God, which are doubtless chastised by these plagues. Thus humility will curb our impatience. And secondly let us consider that it is not for us to remedy these evils; for us it remains only to implore the aid of God in whose hands are the hearts of kings and changes of kingdoms."[1] Both the unhealthy fatalism and the perverse idea that an evil ruler is a divine punishment upon an evil people are not Calvin's own. They run as a constant refrain through all orthodox Christian thought, both Catholic and Protestant, and prove to what degree historic Christianity has been an atrophied prophetic religion in which the force of piety was not properly balanced by a force of spirituality; and the idea of the world as God's creation by the idea of the judgment of God upon the world. In justice to Calvin and Calvinism it must be said that Calvin expressed a more revolutionary sentiment in his sermon on Daniel vi: "We must obey our princes who are set over us, but when they rise against God they must be put down and held of no more account than

---

[1] Calvin's *Institutes*, Book IV, chap. xx.

worn-out shoes. . . . The princes are so intoxicated and be-
witched that they think the world was made for them. When they
seek to tear God from his throne can they be respected? When we
disobey princes to obey him we do no wrong." This word is
important for two reasons. It contains a significant weakness in
that it justifies rebellion against princes only when they commit
some final act of religious pretension, which in Calvin's case meant
that they did not agree with his religion. In modern Germany it
means that the state is resisted only when it tries to make itself
God—*i.e.*, to make itself the source and end of a meaningful
existence. We may be grateful for the ability of historic Christianity to set a final bound beyond which it will not allow political
power to pass and to defend itself heroically against the preten-
tions of the state beyond those bounds. But this is not enough to
establish a dynamic relation between Christianity and politics. A
church which refrains from practically every moral criticism of
the state and allows itself only an ultimate religious criticism of the
spiritual pretensions of the state must logically end in the plight in
which the German Church finds itself.

Calvin's criticism against the princes has another significance. It
opened the sluice for a new type of religious thought in Protestantism in which the theory of the natural law was developed to
justify not only criticism of rulers, but rebellion against them. In
the thought of such men as Beza and John Knox and the Dutch
and American Calvinists this led to a Christian justification of
apolitical rebellion and laid the foundation for a dynamic relationship between Calvinism and the democratic movement. Thus the
implied and covert democracy of Christian conceptions of natural
law finally became explicit and contributed to the overthrow of
monarchy and the establishment of constitutional government.

To complete the indictment against the political confusion of
orthodox Christianity one further fact must be mentioned. Christian perfectionism was often added to theories which were
informed by an undue pessimism on the one hand and an
uncritical piety on the other, and its introduction made confusion
worse confounded. Its real effect was to add weight to the counsel
of acquiescence in injustice. The words of Luther to the rebellious
peasants are prompted by this perfectionism: "Listen dear Chris-

tians to your Christian rights. Thus speaks the supreme Lord whose name ye bear: Ye shall not resist evil, but whosoever shall compel thee to go with him a mile go with him twain and if anyone would have thy coat let him have thy cloak also and whosoever smiteth thee on the right cheek turn to him the other also. Do you hear, you Christian congregation? How does your project agree with this right. You will not bear that anyone will inflict evil or injustice upon you, but you want to be free and suffer only complete justice and goodness."[1] This gratuitous introduction of the principle of non-resistance from a perfectionist ethic into a political ethic of compromise (an idiosyncrasy not only in Luther's thought but in the whole history of orthodoxy) creates the suspicion of a conscious adjustment to class interest. This is particularly true of Luther because no theologian understood the impossibility of the law of love in a world of sin better than he. If some of the political ineptness of Christian orthodoxy must be explained in terms of honest confusions derived from Christian pessimism and Christian piety, the introduction of perfectionist ideas into politics for the purpose of reinforcing counsels of submission to injustice smells of dishonesty. Perhaps it may be regarded as a symbol of the degree to which Christianity became the writing as well as the unwitting tool of class interests.

In the light of this record of the relation of orthodox Christianity to politics the rationalistic and naturalistic rebellion against religion in the eighteenth century must be appreciated as being partly a rebellion of the ethical spirit against religious confusion. The Age of Reason had other and less noble inspirations than this revolt of conscience. It was an age of science which discovered the historical and scientific inaccuracy of religious myth and erroneously imagined that it had given the mythical interpretation of life the *coup de grâce*. It was an age in which the bourgeois spirit first came to flower and lived under the illusion that it represented the ultimate spirituality of human history. It was an age of naturalism which interpreted the flux of history as the ultimate reality, partly because orthodoxy had placed the realm of meaning completely above history and partly because both scientific interest in nature

[1] Luther's *Werke, Gesammtausgabe*, Weimar, vol. xvii, p. 309.

and the scientific conquest of nature prompted the illusion that nature is an adequate home of the human spirit. But all these weaknesses and errors cannot detract from the achievements of the Age of Reason. A prophetic religion which tries to re-establish itself in a new day without appropriating what was true in the Age of Reason will be inadequate for the moral problems which face our generation. Nothing was more natural than the opposition of Voltaire, Diderot, and the Ecyclopaedists to historic religion on the ground that it sanctified injustice. Diderot's confidence that the elimination of "priests and their hypocritical tools" would guarantee a just society was, of course, naïve. The Encyclopaedists did not foresee how quickly one of their disciples would justify Napoleon's imperialism as the "last act in the drama of man's emancipation," nor how deftly the credo of a rationalistic age would be bent to the uses of the capitalistic oligarchs, just as the faith of a pious age was used as a tool of power by the feudal oligarchs.

They were right, nevertheless, in this: Critical intelligence is a prerequisite of justice. Short of the complete identification of life with life which the law of love demands, it is necessary to arbitrate and adjust between competing interests in terms of a critical scrutiny of all the interests involved. Every historic and traditional adjustment of rights must be constantly subjected to a fresh examination. Otherwise the elements of injustice involved in every historic achievement of justice will become inordinate. They will grow not only because it is the tendency of all power and privilege to multiply its demands and pretensions, but also because shifting circumstances will transmute the justice of yesterday into the injustice of tomorrow. Since power is a necessity of social cohesion a rational politics must accept it as a necessary evil. But it must know that it is an evil; and that injustice inevitably flows from its unchecked expression. Consequently any undue piety and reverence for the centres of power is a source of confusion in politics. (Even in so constitutional a monarchy as that of England quasi-religious reverence for the throne was recently used by the Tories of England as a weapon of political conflict.) In so far as religious attitudes have either a constitutional or acquired hostility toward the function of critical intelligence they must be regarded as inimical to justice.

In the same manner, if the force of spirituality in religion and the consequent perfectionism results in an undue pessimism in regard to the immediate possibilities of a higher justice it is the function of reason to explore these possibilities in defiance of traditional religion, just as it is the function of a profound religion to discover the limits of these rational processes and reveal the canker of moral complacency in all moral idealism.

The separation of these functions is unfortunate and unnecessary. It has, in fact, led to the unholy plight of modern culture in which the final insights into the nature of human spirituality contained in historic religion are irrelevant to the specific problems of justice; while the immediate struggle for justice leads to illusions about the total human situation.

Prophetic religion would not only be able to deal more adequately with immediate situations if it were more sympathetic to the function of reason in solving problems of justice. It would also preserve its own vitality and distinctive genius to a greater degree if it allowed rational discrimination to relate the two forces of its faith, gratitude and contrition, to each human situation according to its requirements. Gratitude for the goodness of life and contrition for its evil, the force of piety and that of spirituality, of optimism and pessimism, must be held in balance if prophetic religion is not to atrophy. They cannot be held in balance by some abstract principle. The balance is possible only if each is related to every historic situation with some degree of discrimination. The lack of this discrimination has led the church at times to thank God for the order established by government when it should have resisted tyranny; and at other times to express contrition for sins which resulted in injustice, when it should have moved to change the institutions which generated the injustice.

Historic Christianity is in the position of having the materials for the foundation and the roof of the structure of an adequate morality. But it is unable to complete the structure. Its faith in a meaningful world, having a source beyond itself, is the foundation. Its faith in the end and fulfilment is the roof. The walls, the uprights and diagonals which complete the building are the moral actions and ideals which are fashioned by the application of religion's ultimate insights to all specific situations. This application is a rather sober and prosaic task and a profound religion with its insights into the tragedy of human history and its hope for the ultimate resolution of that tragedy is not always equal to it. Accustomed to a telescopic view of life and history, it does not adjust itself as readily as it might to the microscopic calculations and adjustments which constitute the stuff of the moral life.

6

THE LAW OF LOVE IN POLITICS AND ECONOMICS
Criticism of Christian Liberalism

The effort of the modern Church to correct the limitations of the orthodox Church toward the political order has resulted, on the whole, in the substitution of sentimental illusions for the enervating pessimism of orthodoxy. The orthodox Church dismissed the immediate relevancy of the law of love for politics. The modern Church declared it to be relevant without qualification and insisted upon the direct application of the principles of the Sermon on the Mount to the problems of politics and economics as the only way of salvation for a sick society. The orthodox Church saw the economic order as a realm of demonic forces in which only the most tenuous and tentative order was possible; the modern Church approached the injustices and conflicts of this world with a gay and easy confidence. Men had been ignorantly selfish. They would now be taught the law of love. The Church had failed to teach the law of love adequately because it had allowed the simplicities of the gospel to be overlaid with a layer of meaningless theological jargon. Once this increment of obscurantist theology had been brushed aside, the Church would be free to preach salvation to the world. Its word of salvation would be that all men ought to love one another. It was as simple as that.

Thomas Jefferson stated this faith of the liberal Christianity as well as any liberal theologian: "When we shall have done with the incomprehensible jargon of the Trinitarian arithmetic, that the three are one and the one three, when we shall have knocked down the artificial scaffolding, reared to mask the simple structure of Jesus, when, in short, we shall have unlearned everything which has been taught since his day and got back to the pure and simple doctrines which he inculcated, we shall then be truly and worthily his disciples and my opinion is if nothing had been added to what flowed purely from his lips, the whole world would all this day be Christian."[1] It is fitting that Jefferson, rather than the many theologians of the past two centuries who have repeated such sentiments, should be allowed to state this creed. For Jefferson was a typical child of the Age of Reason; and it is the naïve optimism of the Age of Reason, rather than the more paradoxical combination of pessimism and optimism of prophetic religion, which the modern Church has preached as "the simple gospel of Jesus." The Age of Reason was right in protesting against theological subtleties which transmuted a religion of love into a support of traditional and historic injustice. It was right in assigning an immediate relevance for politics and economics to the law of love and the ideal of brotherhood. In doing that it recaptured some resources of prophetic religion which historic Christianity had lost.

Yet it was wrong in the optimism which assumed that the law of love needed only to be stated persuasively to overcome the selfishness of the human heart. The unhappy consequence of that optimism was to discourage interest in the necessary mechanisms of social justice at the precise moment in history when the development of a technical civilization required more than ever that social ideals be implemented with economic and political techniques, designed to correct the injustices and brutalities which flow inevitably from an unrestrained and undisciplined exercise of economic power.

The purely moralistic approach of the modern Church to politics is really a religio-moral version of *laissez-faire* economics. Jefferson's dictum that the least possible government is the best possible government is a secular version of the faith of the modern Church that justice must be established purely by appeals to the

---

[1] Quoted by T. C. Hall, *The Religious Background of American Culture*, p. 172.

moral ideal and with as little machinery as possible. It would be as unfair to assume that the anarchistic and libertarian assumptions which underlie this belief represent a conscious conformity of the liberal Church to the prejudices of business classes, which have been able to profit from such doctrine, as it would be to accuse Jefferson of devising a political creed for the benefit of his Hamiltonian opponents of the world of finance and industry. It is true, nevertheless, that the plutocracy of America has found the faith of the liberal Church in purely moral suasion a conveniently harmless doctrine just as it appropriated Jeffersonian and *laissez-faire* economic theory for its own purposes, though the theory was first elaborated by agrarian and frontier enemies of big business.

The moralistic utopianism of the liberal Church has been expressed in various forms. Liberal theologians sometimes go to the length of decrying all forms of politics as contrary to Christian spirit of love. Sometimes they deprecate only coercive politics without asking themselves the question whether any political order has ever existed without coercion. Sometimes, with greater realism, they merely declare all forms of violent coercion to be incompatible with the Christian ethic.

In justice to the wing of the liberal Church which has sought to interpret the "social gospel," it must be admitted that it was usually realistic enough to know that justice in the social order could only be achieved by political means, including the coercion of groups which refuse to accept a common social standard. Nevertheless, some of the less rigorous thinkers of the social gospel school tried to interpret the law of love in terms which would rule out the most obvious forms of pressure for the attainment of justice. In one of the best-known social gospel books of the early part of the century Shailer Mathews wrote: "The impulse to get justice is not evangelical; the impulse to give justice is. The great command which Jesus lays upon his followers is not to have their wrongs righted, but to right the wrongs of others." This note of love perfectionism from the gospel is made applicable to the political order without reservation: "Despite the difficulty of realizing its ideal, the emphasis laid by the gospel upon the giving of justice rather than upon the getting of justice is consonant with life as we know it. Revolutions have seldom, if ever, won more rights than the more thoughtful among the

privileged would have been ready to grant."¹ Dr Mathews
partially qualifies this strikingly naïve picture of the political
problem by admitting "that to get justice for others by compelling
the over-privileged to give it to them may be the quintessence of
love, and in so far as the motives of the champions of the
under-privileged are of a sort which the gospel declares to be the
very quality of God."² Unfortunately, this qualification in the
interest of political realism fails to find any place in the Kingdom
of God for the under-privileged themselves who may be fighting
to "get justice." The formula gives moral sanction only to the
kind-hearted "champions of the under-privileged."

Somewhat in the same vein Dr Mathews' colleague, Professor
Gerald Birney Smith, wrote: "The tremendous agitation now
going on in the direction of an appeal to an external and
nonreligious reconstruction is ominous. Does it mean that mankind has become convinced of the impotence of inner spiritual
forces and is willing to trust its case to external reorganization?"³

On the question whether coercion should be used to attain
justice the teaching of the liberal Church, particularly in America,
has been full of confusion. It was impossible for the Church to
escape the fact of coercion or to deny its necessity. Yet it felt that
the Christian gospel demanded uncoerced co-operation. It therefore contented itself, as a rule, with the regretful acceptance of the
fact and necessity of coercion, but expressed the hope that the
Christian gospel would soon permeate the whole of society to such
a degree that coercion in the realm of politics and economics
would no longer be necessary. Shailer Mathews, in a recent book,
which allows the history of the past twenty years to add surpris-
ingly little to his insights of twenty years ago, declares: "There is a
general uncertainty as to whether love and co-operation are a
practical basis upon which to build economic life. . . . Can men
be trusted to co-operate sincerely for their own well-doing or must
groups be coerced into doing that which is to their advantage?"
The question remains unanswered, but is asked again in the same
chapter and answered with a faint hope: "Whether the constructive forces will find capitalist groups sufficiently ready to democ-

---

¹ Shailer Mathews, *The Gospel and the Modern Man*, p. 253.
² *Op. cit.*, p. 255.
³ G. B. Smith, *Social Ideals and the Changing Theology*, p. 145.

ratize privilege and treat wage-earners as partners in the productive process remains to be seen. Humanity does not seem to be naturally generous and the transformation from acquisitiveness to economic co-operation is difficult. The neglect of the principle of sacrifice which Jesus so clearly saw was involved in that personal cooperation which he called love, continues to prevent the betterment of our economic relations." Upon the basis of the slight hope that men will be more loving than they now are Dr Mathews then arrives at the conclusion: "The Christian principle of love applied to economic groups stands over against revolutionary coercion. The Christian movement emphasizes a moral process which does not stand committed to an economic philosophy."[1] Christianity, in other words, is interpreted as the preaching of a moral ideal, which men do not follow, but which they ought to. The Church must continue to hope for something that has never happened. "The success of (industrial) reorganization depends largely upon the readiness of various groups involved to sacrifice profits in the interest of the general good. The fact that such good-will is not fully exhibited explains the need of legal coercion. But the emphasis upon co-operation is another testimony to the validity of the principle of love which Christianity, despite the blundering and selfishness of Christians, has embodied and which it is its mission to evoke."[2]

Francis Peabody, one of the great liberal exponents of social Christianity of the past generation, is even more certain that Dr Mathews that the principles of Jesus are already operative in the industrial world and need only to be extended. He writes: "In spite of insidious temptations in which the world of industry abounds, the spirit and intention of the business world has some contact with the spirit of the teachings of Jesus. The law of service which he announces for his disciples is not a wholly unknown principle in the world of conpetitive trade. It governs the world of industry regarded as a whole. . . . The pillars of modern industrial life are securely set in the moral stability of vast majority of business lives. . . . If any revolution is to overthrow the existing economic system the new order must depend for its permanence

---

[1] Shailer Mathews, *Christianity and Social Progress*, chap. vi.
[2] *Op. cit.*, p. 177.

on the principles of the teachings of Jesus; but if the principles of the teachings of Jesus should come to control the present economic system, a revolution in the industrial order would seem to be unnecessary."[1]

The unvaring refrain of the liberal Church in its treatment of politics is that love and co-operation are superior to conflict and coercion, and that therefore they must be and will be established. The statement of the ideal is regarded as a sufficient guarantee of its ultimate realization. In a recent analysis of the political and economic problem by a British Quaker we read: "The new world must be built upon co-operation and good-will on mutual respect and that sincerity which can face openly and together unpleasant truths. . . . It means in the international order the end of power-politics. . . . We have to exorcise the bullying and hectoring spirit of Palmerston. . . . We have to get rid of the national egoism represented by Bismarck. . . . The old standards of party politics are not good enough for the modern world. . . . It is no longer the prime duty of a party to concentrate upon contentious measure, to appeal to the instincts of pugnacity, to magnify its own credit. It is not the present duty of the opposition to oppose. Its main duty is to offer constructive criticism. . . . If the material well-being of the people is seen to be the purpose industry, the employer and the shareholder will not regard profits as their prerequisite. . . . I believe labourers should try to forget class."[2] Liberal Christian literature abounds in the monotonous reiteration of the pious hope that people might be good and loving, in which case all the nasty business of politics could be dispensed with. In the same vein Church congresses have been passing resolutions for the past decades surveying the sorry state of the world's affairs and assuring the world that all this would be changed if only men lived by the principles of the gospel. Recently the Federal Council of Churches passed resolutions commending the Christian character of Roosevelt's N.R.A. programme, but deprecating the degree of coercion it involved. The implication was that an ideal political programme would depend purely upon voluntary co-operation, of the various economic forces of the nation.

---

[1] Francis Peabody, *Jesus Christ and the Social Question*, pp. 320-326.
[2] H. G. Wood, *The Truth and Error of Communism*, pp. 135-142.

The Buchman movement, supposedly a revitalization of Christianity but in reality the final and most absurd expression of the romantic presuppositions of liberal Christianity, has undertaken to solve all the problems of modern economics and politics by persuading individuals to live in terms of "absolute honesty" and "absolute love." All the ordinary political techniques are disavowed in favour of a voluntary and individualistic love absolutism. The real problems of the political order are understood so little that an apologist for the movement recently recorded the naïve observation: "One of the most helpful facts in speeding the acceptance of the Oxford Group message is that in many lands young and old have grown accustomed to the idea of personal discipline and willingness to sacrifice for the sake of their country."[1]

The sum total of the liberal Church's effort to apply the law of love to politics without qualification is really a curious medley of hopes and regrets. The Church declares that men ought to live by the law of love and that nations as well as individuals ought to obey it; that neither individuals nor nations do; that nations do so less than individuals; but that the Church must insist upon it; that, unfortunately the Church which is to insist upon the law has not kept it itself; but that it has sometimes tried and must try more desperately; that the realization of the law is not in immediate prospect, but the Christian must continue to hope. These appeals to the moral will and this effort to support the moral will by desperate hopes are politically as unrealistic as they are religiously superficial. If the liberal Church had had less moral idealism and more religious realism its approach to the political problem would have been less inept and fatuous. Liberal solutions of the social problem never take the permanent difference between man's collective behaviour and the moral ideals of an individual life into consideration. Very few seem to recognize that even in the individual there is a law in his members which wars against the law that is in his mind.

Sometimes the preacher of hope betrays his realistic fears in spite of his hope. Thus Bishop M'Connell writes: "It seems like the wildest quixotism even to think of trying to get patriotism on

---

[1] Stephen Foot, *Life Began Yesterday.*

the basis of mutual respect between nations. Hitherto the nations have not respected one another. The most hopeless of all tasks is to get nations to a basis of mutual respect. . . . The case seems hopeless, but it must not be allowed to continue so. Just because the situation seems hopeless is a good reason for not allowing the hopelessness to persist. . . . Just think of trying to get a modern nation to bear a cross. Hopeless as the task may appear in dealing with nations, it is not impossible. It calls for a high quality of spiritual attainment admittedly not common even among individuals."[1] These words from one of the really great leaders of the liberal Church fill one with the disquieting feeling that the curious reiteration of despair and hope express the final bankruptcy of the liberal Christian approach to politics. It looks for a moment at the really dark abyss of human sin as it reveals itself particularly in man's collective life, and then edges away. For we must above all continue to hope.

The most perfect swan song of liberal politics has just been written by one of the greatest missionaries of our day, E. Stanley Jones, in his *Christ's Alternative to Communism*. There is a moving fervour and honesty in the book. The communists are establishing an equalitarian society, so runs the argument, by coercion and violence. We must have a just society, but it must be free of political conflict. The only way to beat the communists is to beat them to it. How? By persuading all Christians to live by the law of the Cross. The alternative to revolution is "The Lord's Year of Jubilee . . . men sensibly deciding that it is the only way out, catching the thrill of the new merging of brotherhood, willing to sacrifice to bring it to pass as men were willing to sacrifice during the last war, marching into the new day with a strange new joy. . . . But will men accept it? Yes, I think they will. For two reasons or pressures; disillusionment and desire. . . . The mind of man is becoming more and more latently Christian, perhaps unconsciously so, because of the application of the method of trial and error . . . other methods prove that they invariably lead to chaos. . . . Let men see the Kingdom of God as a really possible way, and the latent Christianity will burst into flame. The Lord's Year of Jubilee may be nearer than we suppose."[2]

---

[1] Francis J. M'Connell, *The Christian Ideal and Social Control*, p. 131.
[2] E. Stanley Jones, *Christ's Alternative to Communism*, p. 169.

Dr Jones' book is such a sincere and moving plea from one of the genuine saints of the missionary movement that one records its complete lack of relevance to the political and economic problems of the hour with regret. Yet its irrelevance is perfectly typical of liberal Christian thought as a whole. Perhaps the actual facts of contemporary politics, the drift toward another world war, the rising tide of tyranny in the nations, driven to desperation by a deepening economic crisis, which are obscured in Dr Jones' sentimental hopes, have been given unconscious recognition in the curious error of his assertion that "the mind of man is becoming more and more latently Christian."

Liberal Christianity has not been totally oblivious to the necessary mechanisms and techniques of social justice in economic and political life. But the total weight of its testimonies has been on the side of sentimental moralism. It has insisted that good-will can establish justice, whatever the political and economic mechanisms may be. It has insisted on this futile moralism at a moment in history when the whole world faces disaster because the present methods of production and distribution are no longer able to maintain the peace and order of society.

Against this moralism it is necessary to insist that the moral achievement of individual good-will is not a substitute for the mechanisms of social control. It may perfect and purify, but it cannot create basic justice. Basic justice in any society depends upon the right organization of men's common labour, the equalization of their social power, regulation of their common interests, and adequate restraint upon the inevitable conflict of competing interests. The health of a social organism depends upon the adequacy of its social structure as much as does the health of the body upon the biochemical processes. No degree of good-will alone can cure a deficiency in glandular secretions; and no moral idealism can overcome a basic mechanical defect in the social structure. The social theories of liberal Christianity deny, in effect, the physical basis of the life of the spirit. They seem to look forward to some kind of discarnate spirituality.

The function of a social mechanism is much more important than liberal Christianity realizes and much more positive than that of acting as a "dyke against sin," as in the view of orthodox Christianity. A profound religion will not give itself to the illusion that perfect justice can be achieved in a sinful world. But neither can it afford to dismiss the problem of justice or to transcend it by premature appeals to the good-will of individuals. Social techniques will not be changed in the interest of justice without the aid of moral incentives. But moral purpose must actually become incorporated in adequate social mechanisms if it is not to be frustrated and corrupted.

Living, as we do, in a society in which the economic mechanisms automatically create disproportions of social power and social privilege so great that they are able to defy and evade even the political forces which seek to equalize and restrain them, it is inevitable that they should corrupt the purely moral forces which are meant to correct them. Christian love in a society of great inequality means philanthropy. Philanthropy always compounds the display of power with the expression of pity. Sometimes it is even used as a conscious effort to evade the requirements of justice, as, for instance, when charity appeals during the Hoover administration were designed to obviate the necessity of higher taxation for the needs of the unemployed. The cynicism of the victims of injustice toward philanthropy is a natural consequence of the inevitable hypocrisy and self-deception which corrupts philanthropy even when its conscious motives are above reproach. There will never be a social order so perfect as to obviate the necessity of perfecting its rough justice by every achievement of social and moral good-will which education and religion may be able to generate. But it must be clearly understood that voluntary acts of kindness which exceed the requirements of coercive justice are never substitutes for, but additions to, the coercive system of social relationships through which alone a basic justice can be guaranteed.

In modern society the basic mechanisms of justice are becoming more and more economic rather than political, in the sense that economic power is the most basic power. Political power is derived from it to such a degree that a just political order is not possible without the reconstruction of the economic order. Specifically this means the reconstruction of the property system. Property has always been power, and inequalities in possession have always made for an unjust distribution of the common social fund. But a technical civilization has transmuted the essentially static disproportions of power and privilege of an agrarian economy into dynamic forces. Centralization of power and privilege and the impoverishment of the multitudes develop at such a pace, in spite of slight efforts at equalization through the pressure of political power upon the economic forces, that the whole system of distribution is imperiled. Markets for the ever increasing flood of goods are not adequate because the buying power of the multitudes is too restricted. Consequently, a periodic glut of goods leads to unemployment crises and general depressions. Efforts to solve this problem, short of the socialization of productive property, lead to a dangerous increase in the power of the state without giving the state final authority over the dominant economic power.

Whatever the defects of Marxism as a philosophy and as a religion, and even as a political strategy, its analyses of the technical aspects of the problem of justice have not been successfully challenged, and every event in contemporary history seems to multiply the proofs of its validity. The political theories of the moralists and religious idealists who try to evade or transcend the technical and mechanical bases of justice are incredibly naïve compared with them. The programme of the Marxian will not create the millennium for which he hopes. It will merely provide the only possible property system compatible with the necessities of a technical age. It is rather tragic that the achievement of a new property system as a prerequisite of basic justice should be complicated by the utopian illusions of Marxism on the one hand and the moralistic evasions of the mechanical problem by liberal Christianity and secular liberalism on the other.

The methods which must be used to achieve such a new property system raises the question of violence and the Christian ethic. An increasing number of Christian liberals, particularly in the left wing of the social gospel movement, have not been as obvious to the mechanics of justice as the main stream of Christian liberalism. From Walter Rauschenbusch to the present day the economic implications of their social theory have been socialistic. But they usually have made one reservation. They have insisted on pacifism in the social struggle. Their arguments in opposition to violence have generally combined many excellent but purely pragmatic scruples against violence with an absolutistic religious objection to it.[1] This confusion of pragmatic with perfectionist scruples is the natural consequence of the lack of clarity in liberal thought about the ethic of Jesus. If Christians are to live by the "way of the Cross" they ought to practice non-resistance. They will find nothing in the gospels which justifies non-violent resistance as an instrument of love perfectionism. They will find only such uncompromising words as "who made me a divider over you." They must recognize that a Christian's concern over his violation of the ethic of Jesus ought to begin long before the question of violence is reached. It ought to begin by recognizing that he has violated the law, "Thou shalt love thy neighbour as thyself." Out of the violation of that commandment arises the conflict of life with life and nation with nation. It is highly desirable to restrict this conflict to non-violent assertions and counter-assertions; but it is not always possible. Sometimes the sudden introduction of a perfectionist ethic into hitherto pragmatic and relative political issues may actually imperil the interests of justice. The Christian who lives in and benefits from, a society in which coercive economic and political relationships are taken for granted, all of which are contrary to the love absolutism of the gospels, cannot arbitrarily introduce the uncompromising ethic of the gospel into one particular issue. When this is done we may be fairly certain that unconscious class prejudices partly prompt the supposedly Christian judgment. It is significant, for instance, that the middle-class Church which disavows violence, even to the degree of frowning upon a strike, is usually composed of people who have enough economic and other forms of covert power to be able to dispense with the more overt forms of violence.

The principal defect of the liberal Christian thought on the question of violence is that it confuses two perspectives upon the problem, the pragmatic and the perfectionist one. Both have their own legitimacy. But moral confusion results from efforts to compound them.

---

[1] Thus, for instance, Professor Bennet in his recent excellent book, *Social Salvation*, lists seven conclusions in regard to the use of violence by Christians. Five of them offer pragmatic scruples against the use of violence, more or less convincing. One justifies participation in social movements if only "incidental" violence occurs. The final conclusion declares "that the way (of the Christian) is the way which prefers to accept the cross to the use of violence against persons."

The attempt to maintain an absolute Christian ethic against the relativities of politics, essentially the strategy of the Christian ascetics, is a valuable contribution to Christian thought and life. We ought to have not only the symbol of the Cross, but recurring historical symbols of the tension between the Christian ideal and the relativities and compromises in which we are all involved. The missionary movement has provided Protestantism with the only symbol of this kind at all comparable to the ascetic movement in Catholicism. Orthodox Protestantism had a theory of justification and grace which invalidated ascetic perfectionism; and liberal Protestantism did not feel the tension of the absolute position sufficiently to produce asceticism. It believed rather in the possibility of living by the law of Christ while remaining related to all the relative and compromising forces of ordinary society. The value of asceticism lies chiefly in its symbolic character. Since the ascetic saint is, economically speaking, a parasite on the sinful world, and since disavowal of the natural relationships and responsibilities of ordinary life leads to the destruction of life itself, his devotion to the absolute ideal can be no more than a symbol of the final ideal of love, under the tension of which all men stand. Yet asceticism is the only possible basis of such perfection. As soon as the family is introduced into the calculations, the absolutist is forced either to a perverse disavowal of natural family obligations or to compromise his perfectionism by protecting the interests of his family more than he would protect merely his own interests. The insistence on celibacy in Catholic asceticism is the product of a profound moral realism. This realism is lacking in every modern religious idealism which thinks it possible to be involved in all the moral relativities, incident upon the defence of limited human groups, beginning with the family and ending with the nation, and yet be true to an absolute ethic by the simple expedient of disavowing violence. Religious pacifism, as a part of a general ascetic and symbolic portrayal of love absolutism in a sinful world, has its own value and justification. A Church which does not generate it is the poorer for its lack. But it ought to be clear about its own presuppositions and understand the conflict between the ideal of love and the necessities of natural life.

A pragmatic pacifism is as justified in its own sphere as a purely religious pacifism, if it is not falsely mixed with the latter. A pragmatic pacifism does not claim the "law of the Cross" as its inspiration. It accepts a world in which interest is set against interest and force against force, and it knows (or ought to know) that in such a world the ideal of the Cross has been violated from the beginning. Its interests lie in mitigating the struggle between contending forces, by insinuating the greatest possible degree of social imagination and intelligence into it and by providing the best possible means of arbitration so that violent conflict may be avoided. Such a pacifism is a necessary influence in every society because social violence is a great evil and ought to be avoided if at all possible. It frequently defeats its own ends. A technical civilization has measurably increased its perils to the whole fabric of civilization and has furthermore increased the hazards of its success as a weapon in the hands of the victims of injustice. When resort is taken to armed conflict, the possessors may have more deadly instruments than the dispossessed. For these and other reasons the avoidance of violence is important in any society, and particularly in the complex society of modern times.

So great are the perils of complete social disintegration, once violence is resorted to, that it is particularly necessary to oppose romantic appeals to violence on the part of the forces of radicalism. But this cannot be done successfully if absolutistic motives are erroneously mixed with a pragmatic analysis of the political problem. The very essence of politics is the achievement of justice through equilibria of power. A balance of power is not conflict; but a tension between opposing forces underlies it. Where there is tension there is potential conflict, and where there is conflict there is potential violence. A responsible relationship to the political order, therefore, makes an unqualified disavowal of violence impossible. There may always be crises in which the cause of justice will have to be defended against those who will attempt its violent destruction. Men may, of course, be mistaken in their devotion to a particular cause and have an erroneous estimate of its relation to the essentials of justice; but that is a possibility in the whole moral and social life. Such a consideration is not an argument against the use of violence, but an important reminder of the relativity of all social issues.

A pragmatic defence of non-violence against romantic appeals to a violent cleansing of the social order would be more effective not only if it remained strictly within the limits of pragmatic and relative canons of the social good, but also if it challenged the real and not the superficial errors of radicalism. Communism is dangerous not so much because it preaches violence, but because it makes so many errors in its analysis of the social problem. Its recognition of the bourgeois origin of democracy leads it to the false conclusion that democracy is purely an instrument of class rule. The fact is that democratic principles and traditions are an important check upon the economic oligarchy, even though the money power is usually able to bend democracy to its uses. The proof that this democratic restraint is still vital is given by the effort of the economic power to abrogate democracy when the latter imperils the rule of the financial oligarchs. This peril of fascism is increased by the unqualified character of the radical cynicism toward democratic institutions. The 1935 meeting of the communist international belatedly recognized this error in communist strategy and sought to amend it. The recognition, however, came too late to save Germany from fascism; and the simplicities of communist dogma will continue to vitiate it as the basis of a new politics. A wise statesmanship will not subordinate its cause to democratic instruments of arbitration, long after the enemy has destroyed their reality (as the German socialists did) but neither will it play into the hands of the enemy by prematurely casting the resources of democracy for orderly social change aside.

Communist romanticism and utopianism are a further hazard to orderly and non-violent social change because it imagines that a pure and anarchistic democracy will grow out of a dictatorship, once the latter has destroyed the capitalistic enemy of democracy. This hope rests upon a totally false analysis of the political problem. It attributes the corruptions of justice solely to capitalistic power and does not recognize that all power is a peril to justice; and that democracy, whatever its limitations, is a necessary check upon the imperialism of oligarchs, whether communistic or capitalistic. The belief that communistic oligarchs have an almost mystical identity of interest with the common man, may seem to justify itself for a brief period in which a radical leadership is kept pure by the traditions of its heroic revolutionary past. But there have been oligarchies with as heroic and sacrificial a tradition in the past. The potency of the tradition hardly outlasts the second generation. The dream of a utopia, to follow a dictatorship once all the enemies of the dictatorship are destroyed, is based upon a failure to discriminate between what is perennial and what is capitalistic in the sources of injustice. This failure increases the tendency to violence in social change because a utopian illusion tempts the proponents of the overthrow of the old system to destructive fury.

A further hazard to orderly change lies in the preoccupation of radicalism with the mechanisms of social life and its inability to appreciate the significance of the organic aspects of society. The organic forces of historic tradition, national sentiment, cultural inheritances, and unconscious loyalties, have a more stubborn vitality than mere social mechanisms, and they may complicate the processes and retard the tempo of social change. The too mechanistic interpretation of society in the typical philosophy of radicalism throws these forces on the side of fascism and leads to false estimates of the intricate processes of social change. The prestige of the Russian example increases this defect in communistic radicalism, because the organic and cultural forces in Russia were so weak that they were easily destroyed with the breakdown of the political and economic structure. A pattern of social change was thus established which is not likely to find a parallel in Western civilization and which confuses the judgment of radical analysts.

These errors of radicalism undoubtedly increase the hazards of social change and tend toward violence. They must be met by a more realistic appraisal of the total social situation. A mere insistence upon the evils of violence is as ineffective against them as homilies on the sinfulness of murder would be in decreasing the homicide rate of a large city.

The avoidance of violence depends not only upon combatting the errors of radicalism, but even more upon dissuading the imperiled wielders of power from a violent defence to their social position, when it is endangered by the rebellious victims of injustice. Since such self-restraint on the part of those who have most to lose is practically impossible to achieve, it would be more accurate to say that the avoidance of social violence depends upon the ability of a wise statesmanship to prevent the lower middle classes and farmers from becoming the political allies of an imperiled capitalistic oligarchy. If those who hold property without possessing essential social power (homes and small savings) are driven, or allow themselves to be beguiled, into the camp of the property-owners, whose property represents essential social power, and in political opposition to the dispossessed, violence in the coming decades of social adjustment will scarcely be avoided. Such a political alignment offers the imperiled oligarchy the fascist alternative to capitulation and increases the desperate fury of the dispossessed. Unfortunately, the classes which have moral scruples against violence are not always particularly helpful in guiding the political thinking of lower middle-class life away from the deceptions and perils of fascist politics.

If the statesmanship of neither radicalism nor liberalism is wise enough to prevent violence in the social changes which are obviously impending in the whole Western civilization, a responsible relation to politics still requires a moral choice between the contending forces. It is hardly necessary to take sides in every social struggle. If no essential issues of justice are at stake in it or if the issues are too confused to justify the hope of any solid gain for the cause of justice, abstention from the conflict may be the only possible course. Such considerations will persuade many to refuse participation in the possible and probable international conflicts which now threaten the peace of the world, even when they do not have perfectionist scruples against participation in social conflict. This type of war-resistance is frequently accused of inconsistency because it does not pledge itself to abstain from internal as well as international struggles. The alleged inconsistency exists only if other than pragmatic reasons are advanced for the refusal to bear arms in international conflict.

This wholly pragmatic and relativistic analysis of the problem of violence obviously fails to arrive at an absolute disavowal of violence under all circumstances. It is therefore tainted with the implied principle that the end justifies the means. This is supposedly a terrible Jesuitical maxim which all good people must abhor. Yet all good people are involved in it. Short of an ascetic withdrawal from the world, every moral action takes place in a whole field of moral values and possibilities in which no absolute distinction between means and ends is possible. There are only immediate and more ultimate values. Whether immediate or ultimate, every value is only partly intrinsic. It is partly instrumental, in the sense that its worth must be estimated in terms of its support of other values. Obviously, any end does not justify any means because every possible value does not deserve the subordination of every other possible value of it. Yet the subordination of values to each other is necessary in any hierachy of values. Freedom, for instance, is a high value which ought not to be too readily or too completely sacrificed for other values. Yet is is sacrificed or subordinated to the necessities of social co-operation. To what degree freedom ought to be subordinated to the requirements of social cohesion, and *vice versa*, is one of those problems for which there is no final answer. It will emerge perennially in human history and be solved according to the requirements, pressures, convictions, and illusions of the hour. Truth is a high value without which the whole structure of social intercourse would disintegrate. Yet even moral purists sacrifice truth, on occasion, to some other high values; they may even sacrifice it to the comparatively dubious end of frictionless social intercourse. No moral purist who holds the doctrine, that the end justifies the means, in abhorrence would fail to make a distinction between a surgeon's violence to the human body and the violence of one who cuts a throat to kill. The distinction would remain valid even if the surgeon's operation resulted in death, as long as death was not the intention but the fortuitous consequence of the operation.

Pacifistic absolutism is sometimes justified by the argument that reverence for life is so basic to the whole moral structure that the sanctity of life must be maintained at all hazards. But even this rather plausible argument becomes less convincing when it is recognized that life is in conflict with life in an imperfect world, and therefore no one has the opportunity of supporting the principle of the sanctity of life in an absolute sense. Fear of the overt destruction of life may lead to the perpetuation of social policies through which human life is constantly destroyed and degraded. How shall one estimate the value of the lives of infants who fall prey to the poverty of an unjust social system against the value of lives which may be sacrificed in a final social crisis? Capital punishment is probably ineffective as a deterrent of murder. But if it were effective its abolition for the sake of the principle of the sanctity of all life would result in an ironical preference of the life of the guilty to that of the innocent.

When dealing with the actual human situation realistically and pragmatically it is impossible to fix upon a single moral absolute. Equal justice remains the only possible, though hardly a precise, criterion of value. Since no life has value if all life is not equally sacred, the highest social obligation is to guide the social struggle in such a way that the most stable and balanced equilibrium of social forces will be achieved and all life will thereby be given equal opportunities of development. But so many contingent factors arise in any calculation of the best method of achieving equal justice that absolute standards are useless. How shall a hazardous method of achieving a predictable social end be measured against a safe method of achieving an unpredictable goal? How shall one gauge the security of the moment against an insecure but promising future? Or how shall one test the validity of any social expectation? To what degree is it illusory and in how far does the illusory element invalidate it? Such questions are not answered primarily by nice rational calculations. They are finally answered through exigencies of history in which contingent factors and unpredictable forces may carry more weight than the nicest and most convincing abstract speculation.

Political problems drive pure moralists to despair because in them the freedom of the spirit must come to terms with the contingencies of nature, the moral ideal must find a proper mechanism for its incarnation, and the ideal principle must be sacrificed to guarantee its partial realization. For the Christian the love commandment must be made relevant to the relativities of the social struggle, even to hazardous and dubious relativities. No doubt prophetic religion must place the inevitable opportunism of statesmanship under a religious prespective. But if we are to have prophetic critics of the statesman may they be prophets who know what kind of a world we are living in and learn how to place every type of statesmanship under the divine condemnation. A prophetic criticism of political opportunism, which mistakes moral squeamishness for religious rigour is easily captured and corrupted by the conservative forces in a social struggle. The "decencies" are usually on the conservative side. The more basic moral values are more likely to rest with the standard of the attacking forces, particularly since human burden-bearers usually have more patience than rebellious heroism and are not inclined to attack established institutions and social arrangments until their situation has become literally intolerable.

7

LOVE AS A POSSIBILITY
FOR THE INDIVIDUAL

No system of justice established by the political, economic, and social coercion in the political order is perfect enough to dispense with the refinements which voluntary and uncoerced human kindness and tenderness between individuals add to it. These refinements are not only necessary, but possible. If the error of the medieval system of politics was to take traditional equilibria of justice for granted without seeking to perfect their basic structure, its virtue was to seek the refinement of this justice by the love of individuals. In spite of the hypocrisies of the traditional medieval "lady bountiful" a genuine humaneness developed within and above the injustices of feudal society which bourgeois society, in spite of its sentimental devotion to the ideals of justice and love, has never achieved. The most grievous mistake of Marxism is its assumption that an adequate mechanism of social justice will inevitably create individuals who will be disciplined enough to "give according to their ability and take according to their need." The highest achievements of social good-will and human kindness can be guaranteed by no political system. They are the consequence of moral and religious disciplines which might be more appreciated in our day if the Christian Church had not mistakenly tried to substitute them for the coercive prerequisites of basic justice.

What is necessary in this respect is also possible. The life of the individual stands in an ascending scale of freedom and therefore under an ascending scale of moral possibilities. An individual who lives in New York does not have the freedom, and therefore lacks the possibility, of relating his life in terms of intimate contact and brotherly obligation to an individual in Tokyo. He is even restrained from that kind of relationship with many people in his own city and his own nation. But there are always areas in which he is free to transcend the mechanisms and the limitations in which all life is involved and to relate his life to other life in terms of voluntary and free co-operation. It must, of course, be remembered that he is not free to transcend the total system of nature in which he stands which sets his life in competition with other life. The command to love his neighbour as himself must, therefore, remain an impossibility as well as a possibility. The ultimate reach of the ideal into the realm of the impossible does not, however, restrict the possibilities. On the contrary it establishes a dimension in which every achievement of human brotherhood suggests both higher and broader possibilities.

A moral discipline calculated to increase the intensity and range of man's obligation to other life involves two factors: The extension of the area in which life feels itself obligated to affirm and protect the interest of other life and the provision of an adequate dynamic to support this obligation. Corresponding to these two factors there are two resources in human nature to which this religio-moral discipline must be related: The natural endowments of sympathy, paternal and filial affection, gregarious impulses and the sense of organic cohesion which all human beings possess, and the faculties of reason which tend to extend the range of these impulses beyond the limits set by nature. Unfortunately, the moral systems which have sought to extend the rational range of social obligation have been deficient in dealing with the problem of social and moral dynamics, while the systems which have dealt with the latter have usually neglected to deal adequately with the rational contribution to morality. On the one side Stoic, Kantian, and utilitarian rationalism have neglected or obscured the problem of moral dynamics, while on the other side Romanticism and many schools of Christian thought have failed to do justice to the contribution of reason to moral conduct. The failure of both schools of moral thought imparts a tragic aspect to the whole history of morality in Western culture.

The rationalists from the Stoics to Kant have correctly assessed the rôle of reason in morality, but have not been able to relate it to the dynamic aspects of life. It is true that reason discloses the "moral law." It reveals, or at least suggests, the total field of life in which obligation moves. The rational man is thus able to recognise the mutual relationships between, let us say, life in Africa and life in America, which the ignorant man does not see and for which he therefore recognizes no obligation. Furthermore, reason discloses how uncontrolled impulses create anarchy both within the self and within the social whole. Against this anarchy it sets the ideal of order. Reason tries to establish a system of coherence and consistency in conduct as well as in the realm of truth. It conceives of its harmonies of life with life not only in ever wider and more inclusive terms, but also works for equal justice within each area of harmony by the simple fact that the special privileges of injustice are brought under rational condemnation for their inconsistency. Under the canons of rational consistency men can claim for themselves only what is genuinely value and they cannot claim value for any of their desires if they are not valuable to others besides themselves. Reason thus forces them to share every privilege except those which are necessary to insure the performance of a special function in the interest of the whole. A large percentage of all special privilege is thereby ruled out by the canons of reason; a fact which persuaded the Enlightenment to expect injustice to vanish with ignorance and has tempted a modern radical rationalist to seek the destruction of social injustice by the simple expedient of puncturing the illusions and prejudices by which social injustice justifies itself in the eyes of both its victims and its beneficiaries.[1] Even utilitarian moral rationalism is not altogether wrong; for on certain levels of conduct reason discloses harmonies of life so immediate and so necessary that only the most heedless egoism will destroy them, since their destruction involves the destruction of the ego's interests.

Reason, in short, discovers that life in its essence is not what it is in its actual existence, that ideally it involves much more inclusive harmonies than actually exist in history. This is what the Stoics meant by the natural law, though neither the Stoics, nor the Age

---

[1] *Cf.* Robert Briffault, *Rational Evolution and Breakdown.*

of Reason after them, were always clear whether natural law wa
the ideal to which reason pointed or certain universally accepte(
standards of conduct in actual history, a confusion which some
times led to a curious compound of radical and conventiona
morality in both cases. Romanticism with its undue and uncritica
emphasis upon the moral dynamic of the emotions failed to d
justice to this critical function of reason in the moral life; an(
Protestant orthodoxy, allowed its idea of total depravity in whicl
man's rationality was involved, to betray it into contempt for th
rational contribution ot morality. Furthermore, reason could onl'
project a law and men could be saved not by law, but by grace
The errors of Romanticism were partially corrected, at least at thi
point, by the Enlightenment; but the error of orthodox Protestant
ism (particularly Lutheran Protestantism) contributed to it:
ineptness in the field of social ethics. The fact is that Christianity
as a whole always had to borrow from some scheme of rationalism
to complete its ethical structure. The early Church borrowed
from Stoicism and Thomasian Catholicism appropriated Aristotelian doctrine to provide a foundation for its more distinctively
Christian superstructure.

In spite of these necessary contributions of reason to moral
conduct and of rationalism to moral theory, no rational moral
idealism can create moral conduct. It can provide principles of
criticism and norms; but such norms do not contain a dynamic for
their realization. In both Stoic and Kantian moral theory the
conflict in the human psyche is mistakenly defined and virtuous
reason is set at variance with the evil impulses. In both cases the
social impulses with which men are endowed by nature are placed
outside of the moral realm. Thus the Stoics regarded the sentiment of pity as evil and in Kantian ethics only actions which are
motivated by reverence for the moral law are good, a criterion
which would put the tenderness of a mother for her child outside
of the pale of moral action.

Rationalism not only supresses the emotional supports of moral
action unduly, but it has no understanding for the problem of
moral dynamics and has, therefore, failed dismally in encouraging
men toward the realization of the ideals which it has projected.
Laws are not automatically obeyed, whether the laws of the state
or the higher law of reason. Henri Bergson criticizes the Stoics for

their inability to produce a morality consistent with their universalistic idealism.[1] In view of the fact that in every system of moral
thought, achievements fall short of ideals, and

> No deed is all its thought had been,
> No wish but feels the fleshly screen,

it may seem unjust to single out the Stoics for condemnation,
particularly when the lives of an Epictetus and a Marcus Aurelius
give a lustre of moral sincerity to a system of thought which the
reputed hypocrisies and dishonesties of a Seneca, Cicero, and
Brutus cannot altogether dim. Nevertheless, it remains true that
Stoicism was unable to arrest the decay of Roman life and that its
idealism was, on the whole, little more than the affectation of a
small intelligent aristocracy.

The effort of various types of rational idealism to provide an
adequate dynamic for their ideal or an adequate theory of
dynamics vary greatly; they are similar only in their common
inadequacy. Utilitarian rationalism sought to use reason to har-
ness egoistic passion to social goals. It thought that the intellectual
demonstration of the intimate inter-relatedness of all life could
persuade men to affirm the interests of their neighbours in
immediate situations out of self-regarding motives. The theory is
absurd because in immediate situations one life may actually live
at the expense of another; in such situations egoistic purpose can
hardly be beguiled by considerations of what life is and ought to
be in its truest and most ultimate essence.

According to the naturalistic rationalism of John Dewey,
reason cuts the channels into which life will inevitably flow
because life is itself dynamic. Reason supplies the direction and
the natural power of life-as-impulse insures the movement in the
direction of the rationally projected goal. The theory presupposes
a non-existent unity of man's impulsive life, a greater degree of
rational transcendence over impulse than actually exists and a
natural obedience of impulse to the ideal which all history refutes.
Nothing in the theory could explain why the nations of the world
are still so far from realizing the rationally projected and univer-

---

[1] Henri Bergson, *Two Sources of Religion and Morality*, p. 52.

sally accepted goal of universal peace.[1] The explanation in terms of the theory would probably be that reason had not yet sufficiently corroded the old tribal behaviour patterns of the nations; but such an explanation hardly does justice to the nontraditional and immediately vital and spontaneous impulses toward war.

If the naturalists among the rationalists think that reason can beguile natural life to extend itself beyond itself, the Kantian idealists can find no effective contact between the real and the ideal world. The intelligible self is the lawgiver and imposes the law of rational consistency: Act so as to make thy action the basis of universal law. But what is to persuade men to obey the law? An inherent force of reverence for law, the sense of obligation. There are two difficulties in this interpretation. One is that the law is only in the realm of essential and not in existential reality. It therefore has no force in the realm of existence to secure its realization. The other error follows naturally from the first: The intelligible self with its sense of obligation is hopelessly cut off from the sensible self of the passions and desires of natural life. The ideal cannot get itself realized; it cannot even enlist the forces of nature in man which inchoately support the ideal.

The failure of Kantian ethics and of rationalistic ethics in general gives the most important clue to importance of the Christian doctrine of love and the Christian faith in God which supports it. Faith in God means faith in the transcendent unity of essence and existence, of the ideal and the real world. The cleavage between them in the historical world is not a cleavage between impulse and reason, though it is by reason that the "law of God" is most fully apprehended. The cleavage can only be mythically expressed as one between obedience and sin, between good-will and evil will. This cleavage is ultimatedly overcome by love. Now love implies an uncoerced giving of the self to the object of its devotion. It is thus a fulfilment of the law; for in perfect love all law is transcended and what is and what ought to be are one. The self is coerced neither by a society to conform to minimal standards nor is it coerced by its other intelligible or rational or ideal self.

---

[1] *Cf.* John Dewey, *Human Nature and Conduct*, pp. 79-83.

Now manifestly this perfect love is, like God, in the realm of transcendence. What relevance does it have, then, to the historical world and what moral action is it able to invoke in human beings in whom "there is a law in their members which wars against the law that is in their minds?" The answer is given in the paradox of the love commandment. To command love is a paradox; for love cannot be commanded or demanded. To love God with all our hearts and all our souls and all our minds means that every cleavage in human existence is overcome. But the fact that such an attitude is commanded proves that the cleavage is not overcome; the command comes from one side of reality to the other, from essence to existence.

The ideal of love is thus first of all a commandment which appeals to the will. What is the human will? It is neither the total personality nor yet the rational element in personality. It is the total organized personality moving against the recalcitrant elements in the self. The will implies a cleavage in the self but not a cleavage primarily between reason and impulse. Consequently, the Christian ideal of a loving will does not exclude the impulses and emotions in nature through which the self is organically related to other life. Jesus therefore relates the love of God to the natural love of parents for their children: "If ye then, being evil, know how to give good gifts unto your children, how much more will your Father which is in heaven give good things to them that ask him?" In its appreciation of every natural emotion of sympathy and pity, of consanguinity and human solidarity, the ethic of Jesus is distinguished from the ethics of rationalism. In this respect there are points of contact between Christianity and Romanticism, perhaps most fully revealed in such men as St Francis. The moral will is not a force of reason imposed upon the emotions. It utilizes whatever forces in nature carry life beyond itself. But since the forces of nature carry life beyond itself only to enslave it again to the larger self of family, race, and community, Christian ethics never has, as in Romanticism, an uncritical attitude toward impulses of sociality. They all stand under the perspective of the "how much more" and under the criticism, "If ye love those who love you what thanks have ye."

The "natural man" is not only under the criticism of these absolute perspectives, but under obligation to emulate the love of

God, to forgive as God forgives, to love his enemies as God loves them. Love as natural endowment, EROS, is transmuted under this religious tension into AGAPE.[1]

In Henri Bergson's *Two Sources of Morality and Religion* the religious force which breaks through the "closed morality" of devotion to family and community is called the force of mysticism. The word mysticism to designate what Bergson has in mind is badly chosen because of the tendency toward passivity and contemplation rather than moral creativity in mysticism, a tendency Bergson himself recognizes but seeks to confine to the eastern rather than Christian mystics.[2] But his idea is correct. The motive power of a love which transcends the impulses of nature is a combination of obedience to God and love of God. The idea of obedience is maintained in Jesus' teachings by the concept of the sovereignty (basileus) of God, usually translated as the "Kingdom of God." The element of obedience, of a sense of moral obligation, of a wilful act of conformity to the divine standard, is consonant with the division between good and evil in the human soul which makes perfect love impossible, because no act is possible in which the resistance of egoism and sin is completely absent. The element of love of God as a motive of social love is consonant with the fact that the attraction of the good is actually present in human life, in spite of its sin. Both the fact that it is present and that it is challenged by sin is expressed in the paradox of the love commandment, "Thou shalt love." In the terms of the moral experience of man it might be stated in the terms, "I feel that I ought to love."

The God, whom to love is thus commanded in the Christian religion is, significantly, the God of mythical-prophetic conception, which means that he is both the ground of existence and the essence which transcends existence. In this mythical paradox lies the foundation for an ethic which enables men to give themselves

---

[1] Professor Anders Nygren in his *Agape and Eros* succinctly states this distinction as developed in Christian theology: "Eros must always regard the love of man as the love for the good in man. . . . Agape is the precise opposite. God's love is the ground and pattern of all love. It consists in free self-giving and it finds its continuation in God's love for man; for he who has received all for nothing is constrained to pass on to others what he has received," p. 171.

[2] *Cf.* Henri Bergson, *op. cit.*, p. 216.

to values actually embodied in persons and existence, but also transcending every actuality thereby escaping both the glorification of human temporal, and partial values characteristic of naturalism and also the morally enervating tendency of mysticism to regard "love of creatures" as disloyalty to God and to confine the love of God to a rational or mystic contemplation of the divine essence which transcends all finite existence. Whatever the weaknesses of Christianity in the field of social morality, history attests its fruitfulness in eliciting loving and tender service to men of all sorts and conditions without regard to some obvious merit which might seem to give them a moral claim upon their fellow-men. The Christian love commandment does not demand love of the fellow-man because he is with us equally divine (Stoicism), or because we ought to have "respect for personality" (Christian liberalism), but because God loves him. The obligation is derived, in other words, not from the obvious unities and affinities of historic existence, but from the transcendent unity of essential reality. The logic of this position is clearly stated by the Quaker saint, John Woolman, in dealing with the question of slavery: "Many slaves on this continent have been oppressed and their cries have reached the ears of the Most High. Such is the purity and certainty of His judgments that he can not be partial to any. In infinite love and goodness he has opened our understanding from time to time, respecting our duty to these people."[1] Naturally such a religious presupposition operates to make men sensitive to the actual underlying unities of human life in historic existence, as expressed, for instance, in the words of St Paul: "He hath made of one blood all the races of men." But the obligation is derived from a more transcendent unity and purity of value than any historic realities, and is therefore proof against the disappointments and disillusions of naturalistic morality, in which there is always a touch of a romantic exaggeration of the goodness of man and a corresponding cynical reaction. But the insistence upon the Creation as a work of God always saves prophetic religion from contempt for the partial and imperfect values of history and a consequent identification of religion with a passive contemplation

---

[1] Gummere, *Journal of John Woolman*, p. 216.

of a transcendent ideal beyond existence. Unfortunately, historic Christianity has sometimes been partially beguiled from this prophetic position, as, for instance, in the theology of Thomas Aquinas in which Aristotelian rationalism influences him to regard a rational and mystical contemplation of the divine as religiously superior to ethical action.

The Christian doctrine of love is thus the most adequate metaphysical and psychological framework for the approximation of the ideal of love in human life. It is able to appropriate all the resources of human nature which tend toward the harmony of life with life, without resting in the resources of "natural men." It is able to set moral goals transcending nature without being lost in other-worldliness. The degree of approximation depends upon the extent to which the Christian faith is not merely a theory, but a living and vital presupposition of life and conduct. The long history of Christianity is, in spite of its many failures, not wanting in constant and perennial proofs that love is the fruit of its spirit. Martyrs and saints, missionaries and prophets, apostles and teachers of the faith, have showed forth in their lives the pity and tenderness toward their fellow-men which is the crown of the Christian life. Nor has Christianity failed to impart to the ordinary human relations of ordinary men the virtues of tenderness and consideration.

While every religion, as indeed every human world view, must finally justify itself in terms of its moral fruits it must be understood that the moral fruits of religion are not the consequence of a conscious effort to achieve them. The love commandment is a demand upon the will, but the human will is not enabled to conform to it because moralistic appeals are made to obey the commandment. Moralistic appeals are in fact indications of the dissipation of primary religious vitality. Men cannot, by taking thought, strengthen their will. If the will is the total organized personality of the moment, moving against recalcitrant impulse, the strength of the will depends upon the strength of the factors which enter into its organization. Consequently, the acts and attitudes of love in which the ordinary resources of nature are supplemented are partly the consequence of historic and traditional disciplines which have become a part of the socio-spiritual inheritance of the individual and partly the result of concatenations of circumstance in which the pressure of events endows the individual with powers not ordinarily his own.

The soldier's courage, his ability to transcend the inclination of "natural man" to flee death, is the fruit of a great tradition and the spirit of the military community which enforces it. In the same manner the tenderness and graciousness with which men are able to regard the problems of their fellow-men, beyond the natural inclinations of human nature, is the fruit of a religio-moral tradition and the loyalty of a religious community to the tradition. Even if we cannot accept St Paul's Christ-mysticism, bordering as it does on the very edge of the magical, it is nevertheless true that the Church is the body of Christ and that the noble living and the noble dead in her communion help to build up in her the living Christ, a dimension of life which transcends the inclinations of natural man. It is consequently natural and inevitable that the faithful should regard genuine acts of love as proceeding from propulsions which are not their own, and should confess with St Paul, "I, yet not I, but Christ that liveth in me."

Sometimes the act of complete self-abnegation, the pouring out of life for other life, is the consequence of pressures of a given moment which endow the individual with resources beyond his natural capacities. The mother who sacrifices her life for her child is enabled to do this by the heightening of the natural impulses of mother love in a moment of crisis. In soberer moments of reflection she could not give herself so completely for another life. The same mother who thus sacrifices herself might conceivably be engaged in more prosaic moments in shrewd unconscious calculations in which mother love is compounded with the will-to-power. Martyrs do not achieve martyrdom by taking thought. Whether a man stands or yields in the hour of crisis is of course determined by commitments made before the crisis arises. Devotion to a cause may be such that it becomes irrevocable and its revocation would result in the complete disintegration of personality. The crisis with its impending martyrdom adds its emotional pressures to the commitment of previous years. Furthermore, a strong devotion to a cause absorbs the individual in the cause so that the entire socio-spiritual impetus of the enterprise sustains him in the hour of crisis and endows him with resources which transcend anything possessed in his own right.

The Catholic doctrine that faith, hope, and love are "theological" virtues which are added to the moral possibilities of natural man by an infusion of grace is thus, broadly speaking, true to the facts. Only it is not true that the grace which is added is necessarily infused by the sacraments nor even that the Christian faith is its only possible presupposition. The grace of God is not confined so narrowly as theological defenders of historic religious institutions would like to confine it. But there are, nevertheless, forces in life which can only be described as the grace of God. What men are able to will depends not upon the strength of their willing, but upon the strength which enters their will and over which their will has little control. All moral action really stands under the paradox: "Work out your salvation in fear and trembling; for it is God who worketh in you both to will and to do his good pleasure."

But love is not only a fruit of grace, but also a fruit of faith; which is to say that the total spiritual attitude which informs a life determines to what height a moral action may rise in a given moment. Deeds of love are not the consequence of specific acts of the will. They are the consequence of a religio-moral tension in life which is possible only if the individual consciously lives in the total dimension of life. The real motives of love, according to the Christian gospel, are gratitude and contrition. Gratitude and contrition are the fruits of a prophetic faith which knows life in its heights and in its depths. To believe in God is to know life in its essence and not only in its momentary existence. Thus to know it means that what is dark, arbitrary, and contingent in momentary existence can neither be accepted complacently nor tempt to despair.

To understand life in its total dimension means contrition because every moral achievement stands under the criticism of a more essential goodness. If fully analyzed the moral achievement is not only convicted of imperfection, but of sin. It is not only wanting in perfect goodness, but there is something of the perversity of evil in it. Such contrition does not destroy selfishness in the human heart. But there is a difference between the man who understands something of the mystery of evil in his own soul and one who complacently accepts human egoism as a force which must be skilfully balanced with altruism in order that moral unity may be achieved.

To understand life in its total dimension means to accept it with grateful reverence as good. It is good in its ultimate essence even when it seems evil and chaotic in its contingent and momentary reality. Faith in its essence is not an arbitrary faith. Once held, actual historic existence verifies it; for there are in life as we know it in history and nature innumerable symbols of its ultimate and essential nature. Grateful reverence toward the goodness of life is a motive force of love in more than one sense. Gratitude for what life is in its essence creates a propulsive power to affirm in existence what is truly essential, the harmony of life with life. Furthermore, under the insights of such a faith, the fellow-man becomes something more than the creature of time and place, separated from us by the contingencies of nature and geography and set against us by the necessities of animal existence. His life is seen under the aura of the divine and he participates in the glory, dignity and beauty of existence. We do not love him because he is "divine." If that pantheistic note creeps into prophetic faith it leads to disillusion. He is no more divine than we are. We are all imbedded in the contingent and arbitrary life of animal existence and we have corrupted the harmless imperfections of nature with the corruptions of sin. Yet we are truly "children of God" and something of the transcendent unity, in which we are one in God, shines through both the evil of nature and the evil in man. Our heart goes out to our fellow-man, when seen through the eyes of faith, not only because we see him thus under a transcendent perspective but because we see ourselves under it and know that we are sinners just as he is. Awed by the majesty and goodness of God, something of the pretence of our pretentious self is destroyed and the natural cruelty of our self-righteousness is mitigated by emotions of pity and forgiveness.

The moral effectiveness of the religious life thus depends upon deeper resources than moral demands upon the will. Whenever the modern pulpit contends itself with the presentation of these demands, however urgent and fervent, it reveals its enslavement to the rationalistic presuppositions of our era. The law of love is not obeyed simply by being known. Whenever it is obeyed at all, it is because life in its beauty and terror has been more fully revealed to man. The love that cannot be willed may nevertheless grow as a natural fruit upon a tree which has roots deep enough to be nurtured by springs of life beneath the surface and branches reaching up to heaven.

8

LOVE AS FORGIVENESS

The crown of Christian Ethics is the doctrine of forgiveness. In it the whole genius of prophetic religion is expressed. Love as forgiveness is the most difficult and impossible of moral achievements. Yet it is a possibility if the impossibility of love is recognized and the sin in the self is acknowledged. Therefore an ethic culminating in an impossible possibility produces its choicest fruit in terms of the doctrine of forgiveness, the demand that the evil in the other shall be borne without vindictiveness because the evil in the self is known.

Forgiveness is a moral achievement which is possible only when morality is transcended in religion. No pure morality can bridge the gap which divides men according to their conflicting interests and their natural, racial, and geographic backgrounds, because their moral idealism is conditioned by these very factors. The fact that it is really a moral idealism and not purely a selfish or partial interest which motivates them makes them more secure in their self-respect and therefore more ruthless against their foes. One reason why modern social conflicts are more brutal than primitive ones is that the development of rationality has actually imparted more universal pretensions to partial social interests than those of primitive men, and yet has stopped short of transmuting any partial interest into one of genuine universal validity. The consequence is that modern men fight for their causes with a fury of which only those are capable who are secure in the sense of their righteousness. Thus all modern social conflicts are fought for

"Kultur," for democracy, for justice, and for every conceivable universal value. A rereading of the pronouncements of the men of learning and philosophers, as well as of the statesmen and politicians, who were involved in the world war, fills the reader with a depressing sense of the calculated insincerity of all their pretensions. Yet while some of the sentiments were no doubt brazenly insincere and calculated to deceive the public, many of them were merely a striking revelation of the pathos of modern spirituality.

The effort of modern secularism to solve this problem is perfectly stated in Professor John Dewey's recent exposition of his religious faith.[1] He would eliminate conflict and unite men of good-will everywhere by stripping their spiritual life of historic, traditional, and supposedly anachronistic accretions. This proposal is a striking example of the faith of modern rationalism in the ability of reason to transcend the partial perspectives of the natural world in which reason is rooted. Every event in contemporary history proves that modern idealists are divided from each other by something more vital and immediate than anachronistic religious traditions. Modern communism and modern nationalism are both religions, both modern, and both maintained by a demonic fervour in which partial perspectives and devotion to a high ideal are compounded. Where is the rationality which will resolve or modify this fervour? Perhaps it may be found among a small group of intellectuals whose intellectual idealism is rooted in the comparative neutrality and security of the intellectual life.

There is no deeper pathos in the spiritual life of man than the cruelty of righteous people. If any one idea dominates the teachings of Jesus, it is his opposition to the self-righteousness of the righteous. The parable spoken unto "certain which trusted in themselves that they are righteous, and despised others"[2] made the most morally disciplined group of the day, his Pharisees, the object of his criticism. In fact, Jesus seems to have been in perpetual conflict with the good people of his day and ironically justified his consorting with the bad people by the remark that not those who are whole, but those who are sick, are in need of a

---

[1] John Dewey, *A Common Faith*.
[2] *Luke xviii.* 9.

physician. The Christian tradition, partly under the influence of the conflict between the early church and the synagogue, echoes of which have coloured the gospel narratives, has pictured the Pharisees as particularly brazen hypocrites. This tradition probably betrays an unconscious effort to avoid self-accusation on the part of the good people in the Christian Church through all the ages. The strictures against the Pharisees would apply with equal validity to any moral aristocracy of any age.

The criticism which Jesus levelled at good people had both a religious and a moral connotation. They were proud in the sight of God and they were merciless and unforgiving to their fellow-men. Their pride is the basis of their lack of mercy. The unmerciful servant, in Jesus' parable is unforgiving to his fellow-servant in spite of the mercy which he had received from his master. Forgiving love is a possibility only for those who know that they are not good, who feel themselves in need of divine mercy, who live in a dimension deeper and higher than that of moral idealism, feel themselves as well as their fellow men convicted of sin by a holy God and know that the differences between the good man and the bad man are insignificant in his sight. St Paul expresses the logic of this religious feeling in the words: "With me it is a very small thing that I should be judged of you or of man's judgment: yea, I judge not mine own self. For I know nothing by myself; yet am I not thereby justified: but he that judgeth me is the Lord."[1] When life is lived in this dimension the chasms which divide men are bridged not directly, not by resolving the conflicts on the historical levels, but by the sense of an ultimate unity in, and common dependence upon, the realm of transcendence. For this reason the religious ideal of forgiveness is more profound and more difficult than the rational virtue of tolerance.

Tolerance is, no doubt, an important rational and moral achievement. It is actually possible for an intelligent person to appreciate the merits of an opponent's position to a degree impossible for the ignorant devotee. Yet tolerance tends to become dissipated as soon as the impartial observer is forced by the exigencies of history to espouse one side or the other. The observation of G. K. Chesterton, that tolerance is the virtue of

---

[1] 1 Corinthians iv. 3-4.

people who do not believe in anything, is fairly true. The ideal of tolerance in modern liberalism, for instance, lasted only in the expansive period of capitalism during which the social struggle was not acute. The oligarchs could espouse the ideal or tolerance because their power was not challenged and the intellectuals could espouse it because social stability created a large area of social neutrality from the vantage-point of which conflicting movements and contrasting creeds could be surveyed with impartiality. But the sharpening social struggle in Europe has almsot completely destroyed the ideal of tolerance of traditional liberalism. It is significant that in Germany, where the processes of modern life are most advanced, secular liberalism has been completely destroyed. Only the churches, which the secular liberals of yesterday regarded as anachronistic institutions have been able to preserve some of the humanities in the terrible social tension to which that nation is being subjected. The recent history of Germany gives point to the observation of Irving Babbitt:

"The honest thinker, whatever his own preferences, must begin by admitting that while religion can get along without humanism, humanism cannot get along without religion. The reason has been given by Burke in pointing out the radical defect in Rousseau. The whole ethical life has its roots in humility. As humility diminishes, conceit and vain imaginings rush in almost automatically to take its place."[1]

Yet it might be claimed that a forgiving attitude toward the foe is no more possible than a tolerant one, except perhaps by a strategy of declaring all moral and social issues upon which men are divided to be irrelevant not only from a divine but from an historical perspective. In that case it might be possible but not desirable. This fact confronts Christian ethics with a problem for which there is no easy solution. A religious ethic, like that of Tolstoi, which makes forgiveness of the foe a substitute for socio-moral action, is full of danger. In Russia Tolstoi's absolutism deflected a promising movement of political reform. Equally dangerous is the emphasis of modern dialectical theology upon the irrelevance of moral and social issues. The victim of injustice cannot cease from contending against his oppressors,

---

[1] *Rousseau and Romanticism*, p. 380.

even if he has a religious sense of the relativity of all social positions and a contrite recognition of the sin in his own heart. Only a religion full of romantic illusions could seek to persuade the Negro to gain justice from the white man merely by forgiving him. As long as men are involved in the conflicts of nature and sin they must seek according to best available moral insights to contend for what they believe to be right. And that will mean that they will contend against other men. Short of the transmutation of the world into the Kingdom of God, men will always confront enemies; and the enmity between man and man will be rooted not only in the divisions which nature has created, but in the idealisms which men have erected upon these divisions.

Forgiveness in the absolute sense is therefore an impossibility as much as any other portion of Christ's perfectionism. If one were to follow the words of Jesus, "Let him who is without sin cast the first stone," without qualification, no criminal could ever be arrested. Every society which punishes its anti-social members is more responsible for their anti-social conduct than it realizes. But it is not possible to desist from all forms of social punishment when this responsibility is realized. Yet it is possible to deal with the criminal in terms of this realization and to qualify the spiritual pride of the usually self-righteous guardians of public morals. In the same way is it possible to engage in social struggles with a religious reservation in which lie the roots of the spirit of forgiveness.

The spirit of forgiveness in social conflict does not depend upon the ability of men to reach an absolute perspective which transcends the conflict. The pretension that they are able to do this is the very tendency toward the demonic which imparts such a pathos to all human history. They need only to know that there is a transcendent perspective from which "all our righteousnesses are as filthy rags." Implied in such a faith is the sense of a goodness which not only fulfils, but may negate, the highest human goodness. This is the implication developed in the Book of Job, when God refuses to be judged by human standards of justice and quiets the protests of Job by overawing him with the mysteries of the world beyond human ken.

It cannot be denied that such a faith is dangerous to morality. It may tempt men to blunt the sharpness of moral distinctions which must be made in human history. But it is as necessary as it is dangerous. Without it men always construct God not only in terms of the universally human, but in terms of particular and partial human perspectives, and thereby increase the fury of their self-righteousness. The ultimate paradox of a genuine theism is that only its supramoral pinnacle is able to save its moral values from degeneration. The merit of such a faith lies not only in its destruction of human pretension, but also in its guarantee against religious disillusionment. A too strongly humanistic theism cannot possibly comprehend the whole world into its universe of meaning, because there are processes in nature which are in obvious conflict with the highest human purposes. Such a theism, therefore, tends to perpetual dissolution into a humanistic dualism in which man is persuaded to rebel against the world as nothing more than "the trampling march of unconscious power." A genuine prophetic faith reaches a transcendence in which the conflict between man and nature is overcome, even when the conflict defies every effort of rational comprehension.

It is an instructive fact that our age, which began with the substitution of humanism for theism as a more direct and unambiguous method of protecting human values, ends in a series of international and fratricidal struggles in which the common human dignity of man is outraged. Amid such struggles men as men have no rights at all. Their humanity is recognized only in its functional relationship to the national or other political cause to which they are related. Fascists and communists not only destroy one another, but subject each other to tortures and cruelties which a common respect for human life ought to make impossible. A humanism which is sustained only by the obvious marks of common humanity breaks down when the hysteria of conflict destroys or obscures these obvious human ties. The humanities, which secularism tries to preserve as ultimate ends and as self-sufficient values, literally depend upon a structure of value which reaches beyond them. A universe of value in which there is no dimension of depth is rent asunder along its thin surfaces by the forces of nature and history if it is not held together in a larger universe, the heights of which transcend the conflicts of the moment.

Historic Christianity has frequently been no more successful than secularism in subjecting historic and partial human perspectives and moral values to the scrutiny of the Absolute. The fact is that the tendency toward the religious sanctification of partial values is so powerful that no religion, no matter how potent its presuppositions, escapes. The very division of Christianity into various denominations, churches, and sects is a consequence of the influence of relative historical forces upon the universally valid presuppositions of a prophetic faith. Catholicism is the form which Christianity has taken in the Latin and Slav countries, on the one hand, and in the feudal structure of society, on the other. In spite of its universal pretensions (and universal achievements beyond those of Protestantism) it is today, particularly in Spain, Latin America and in the Latin world generally, the spiritual façade behind which a decaying feudal social structure seeks to hide its shabbiness and through which it tries to achieve a measure of spiritual dignity. The Catholic doctrine of the Church is, in fact, a constant temptation to demonic pretensions, since it claims for an institution, established in time and history, universal and absolute validity. Except for the fact that its institution is actually more universal than a single state, this Catholic claims leads to reactionary political consequences, similar to those of Hegelianism, in which the Absolute is thought to be incarnate in a single state. Considering the tremendous perils of these religious pretensions, Marx is quite right in asserting that "the beginning of all criticism is the criticism of religion."

Protestant theory does not give the historic and concrete institution the same aura of the Absolute. It does not identify the Church with the Kingdom of God, nor the historic Church with the Church of Christ. The real Church is always in the sphere of transcendence. In spite of this difference, Protestantism has frequently lent itself to the religious sanctification of partial values more adjectly than Catholicism. The actual universal structure of the historic institution in Catholicism has saved it from some of these errors of Protestantism. Thus Protestantism in Germany was much more definitely the interest of a particular class than Catholicism, which actually mitigated the intensity of the social struggle and avoided the peril of becoming the instrument of reaction against the forces of social radicalism. The thesis that Protestantism in general and Calvinism in particular had something of the same intimate relationship with capitalism, which existed between Catholicism and feudalism, is now a quite generally accepted presupposition of historic interpretation in spite of the modifications to which the theory has been subjected since Max Weber first propounded it. The relationship of Protestantism and Catholicism to the political dispute between the southern and northern Irish, a dispute to which both economic and Scotch-Irish racial antagonisms contribute, reveals either form of Christianity equally enmeshed in the political conflicts of national, racial, and economic groups. Religion has been, in fact, so perennially involved in, and has served to accentuate, such disputes that a secular age thought it possible to eliminate the disputes by destorying religion. It failed to realize that all wars are religious wars, whether fought in the name of historic creeds or not. Men do not fight for causes until they are "religiously" devoted to them; which means not until the cause seems to them the centre of their universe of meaning. This is just as true in a supposedly secular age as in an avowedly religious one.

It must be admitted, therefore, that historic Christianity, in common with other religions, usually succumbs to the parochialism of the human heart and lends itself to the sinful inclination of human groups to make themselves God. The critics of Christianity, or of religion in general, are wrong only in attributing this tendency to some defect in Christianity itself or in the character of religion, and in not realizing with how basic a difficulty of human spirituality they are dealing.

Whatever the delinquencies of historic Christianity in this matter, there is no question but that the essential genius of the Christian faith is set against the religious sanctification of partial and relative values. The very rise of prophetic religion is to be found in the criticism by the eighth-century Hebrew prophets of the absolute religious claims made by their race and nation. The prophets insisted that the same God who had called Israel to be his people might also judge them and destroy them. Historic religion is not frequently true to this religious perspective. Nor is it easy to be true to it and yet remain in responsible relationship to the various historic human enterprises in which men seek to establish relative justice amidst the confusion and controversy of social life.

Loyalty to such a faith requires a responsible relationship and devotion to whatever cause seems most likely to achieve the highest measure of relative justice; but also the spirit of forgiveness in the struggles in which such a cause becomes involved. Genuine forgiveness is not a frequent achievement in individual relationships. It is naturally even more rare in collective relationships. But it is not impossible, because the consciouness of sin within the self, even while the self contends against the sin of others, is a natural consequence of any really thoroughgoing analysis of life. The superficialities of modern culture have not predisposed modern man to such an analysis. He has consequently taken a complacent attitude toward the forces of anarchy which reside in the human soul. But what is hidden becomes revealed. Contemporary historical events must finally persuade the modern soul how little its complacency conforms to the perilous facts of human existence.

In the inevitable struggles through which this generation must pass before its civilization can achieve any measure of health, it will be more important to preserve the spirit of forgiveness amidst the struggles than to seek islands of neutrality. The very breadth of social cohesion in a technical social order has made such islands extremely narrow, so that they afford little or no protection against the waves of party strife which periodically inundate them. If the humanities are preserved at all they will be preserved only to the degree that the resources of a profound and prophetic religion will inform the spirit of modern man so that he may look at the confusion of his day without despair and seek to coerce its anarchy into some new order without the fury of self-righteousness.

The spirit of modern man is much too seriously corrupted by the romantic substitutes for a prophetic faith, inherited from the past two centuries of "emancipation," to justify the hope that a prophetic interpretation of life will wield a potent influence in contemporary history. There will be occasions when it will be able to speak a decisive word and there are localities and nations in which its influence will perceivably mitigate the fury of the social struggle. On the whole it will have no more influence in a secular age than humanism had in an age when religion had degenerated to magic. Yet the humanism of the Middle Ages was an exceedingly important seed corn for all that was good in the history of Western culture.

"If hopes are dupes, fears may be liars," and it may be that the insights of a prophetic religion may qualify and mitigate the cruelties of the social struggles through which we are passing to a greater degree than now seems probable. It is comforting to know, nevertheless, that if this should not prove true, the truth of prophetic religion, and of Christianity in so far as Christianity is truly prophetic, must survive the tempests of a dying civilization as an ark surviving the flood. At some time or other the waters of the flood will recede and the ark will land. Human life can have dignity only as it is comprehended and understood in a universe of meaning which transcends human life. It is the life in this ark of prophetic religion, therefore, which must generate the spirituality of any culture of any age in which human vitality is brought under a decent discipline.

Since the anarchy of human life is something more than the anarchy of animal existence, it cannot be checked by the forces inherent in a rational culture. The vitality, and the resulting anarchy of human existence, is the vitality of children of God. Nothing short of the knowledge of the true God will save them from the impiety of making themselves God and the cruelty of seeing their fellow men as devils because they are involved in the same pretension.

INDEX